The

CONSTITUTION

of the

UNITED STATES *of* AMERICA

with the

DECLARATION

of

INDEPENDENCE

The

CONSTITUTION

of the

UNITED STATES *of* AMERICA

The

DECLARATION

of

INDEPENDENCE

CASTLE
BOOKS

Brimming with creative inspiration, how-to projects, and useful information to enrich your everyday life, Quarto Knows is a favorite destination for those pursuing their interests and passions. Visit our site and dig deeper with our books into your area of interest: Quarto Creates, Quarto Cooks, Quarto Homes, Quarto Lives, Quarto Drives, Quarto Explores, Quarto Gifts, or Quarto Kids.

Inspiring | Educating | Creating | Entertaining

This edition published in 2014 by

CASTLE BOOKS ®
an imprint of The Quarto Group
142 West 36th Street, 4th Floor
New York, New York 10018
USA
www.QuartoKnows.com

© 2014 Quarto Publishing Group USA Inc.

ISBN: 978-0-7858-3251-5

Design by S. E. Livingston

Cover Image: Library of Congress,
Prints & Photographs Division, LC-DIG-ppmsca-34637

Printed in China
8 10 9

MIX
Paper from
responsible sources
FSC® C016973
www.fsc.org

CONTENTS

INTRODUCTION

On July 4, 1776, in the midst of the Revolutionary War, the thirteen original colonies of the United States ratified a document that would later be known as the Declaration of Independence. In it, the Continental Congress and the people it represented declared they were no longer under the rule of Great Britain and were now the United States of America.

This newly formed country had one of its most respected citizens write the Declaration, thirty-three-year-old Virginia delegate Thomas Jefferson. Though he was one of the youngest members of the Congress, his fellow members of the Declaration committee quickly chose him to draft this important document. When Jefferson suggested John Adams instead, Adams gave him the reasons he was the best choice: "Reason first—You are a Virginian, and a Virginian ought to appear at the head of this business. Reason second—I am obnoxious, suspected, and unpopular. You are very much otherwise. Reason third—you can write ten times better than I can." Jefferson spent two and a half weeks writing and rewriting what would become the defining treatise of his legacy. His words still resonate with Americans and people all over the world who believe in an individual's right to "life, liberty and the pursuit of happiness."

Soon after the Declaration of Independence was signed, a second Continental Congress convened to draft the Articles of Confederation, which dealt with matters of war and state sovereignty. But after the Revolutionary War, a document was needed to form a stronger union and to provide a permanent guarantee of the political liberties achieved during the Revolution.

The Delegates who convened at the Federal Convention in Philadelphia on May 25, 1787, quickly rejected the idea of revising the Articles of Confederation and agreed to construct a new framework for a national government. Throughout the next four months, they debated the proper form such a government should take, led by their elected president, George Washington.

Few of the delegates questioned the need to establish a more vigorous government to preside over the union of states. It was recognized by most in the land that the Articles of Confederation failed to provide the federal government with the authority to raise revenue, regulate commerce, or enforce treaties.

The challenging task before the delegates was to create a government that could encompass the thirteen existing states and accommodate the anticipated expansion to the west. The resulting document's distribution of authority between legislative, executive, and judicial branches was a boldly original attempt to create a robust central government while preserving the independence of individual states and their citizens.

The longest debate of the convention centered on representation in the Congress. The division between representatives from the smaller states, which thought all states should have equal representation, and the larger states, which proposed representation proportional to population, threatened to bring the proceedings to a halt. Over several weeks, the delegates developed a complicated compromise that provided for equal representation of the states in a Senate (elected by state legislatures) and a House of Representatives, elected by popular vote.

But perhaps more contentious was an undercurrent of conflict during the debates between the slave states and the free states. The Constitution ultimately granted protection to the institution of slavery, even though it never overtly mentions the word "slavery." This strained attempt at compromise would remain unresolved until 1865, when the Thirteenth Amendment, abolishing slavery, was passed.

The need for amendments to the Constitution had come along much earlier than that, however—in fact, the debates that ensued in state senates while the Constitution was being ratified by each state made clear the need for additions to the basic framework drafted in Philadelphia. Beginning with Massachusetts, a number of state conventions ratified the Constitution with the request that text be written to protect certain liberties at the core of American traditions.

James Madison, a longtime friend and colleague of Declaration writer Thomas Jefferson, was by then a member of the new United States House of Representatives, and set about making changes to the Constitution to guarantee the freedoms that Americans hold dear. But several of his fellow representatives objected, especially well-respected Connecticut representative Roger Sherman, who said that Congress had no authority to change the Constitution directly. So Madison drafted a list of amendments that would come to be known as the Bill of Rights.

These amendments (which were ratified in 1791) and those that have followed have enabled the Constitution to adapt to changing conditions in American society all while keeping the founders' basic outline of national government intact.

The documents in this collection, the Declaration of Independence and the Constitution of the United States of America, are a monument to the combined spirit of all Americans as well as a testament to the extraordinary minds of our founding fathers, who put them on paper. A full, analytical index of the original Constitution and all of its ratified amendments follows.

THE
DECLARATION
OF INDEPENDENCE

IN CONGRESS, JULY 4, 1776

The Unanimous Declaration of the Thirteen United States of America

When in the Course of human events, it becomes necessary for one people to dissolve the political bands which have connected them with another, and to assume among the powers of the earth, the separate and equal station to which the Laws of Nature and of Nature's God entitle them, a decent respect to the opinions of mankind requires that they should declare the causes which impel them to the separation.

We hold these truths to be self-evident, that all men are created equal; that they are endowed by their Creator with certain unalienable rights; that among these are Life, Liberty, and the pursuit of Happiness; that, to secure these rights, governments are instituted among Men, deriving their just powers from the consent of the governed; that whenever any form of government becomes destructive of these ends, it is the right of the people to alter or to abolish it, and to institute new government, laying its foundation on such principles, and organizing its powers in such form, as to them shall seem most likely to effect their safety and happiness. Prudence, indeed, will dictate that governments long established should not be changed for light and transient causes; and accordingly all experience hath shown that mankind are more disposed to suffer, while evils are sufferable than to right themselves by abolishing the forms to which they are accustomed. But when a long train of abuses and usurpations, pursuing invariably the same object, evinces a design to reduce them under absolute despotism, it is their right, it is their duty, to throw off such government, and to provide new guards for their future security. Such has been the patient sufferance of these colonies; and such is now the necessity which constrains them to alter their former systems of government. The history of the present King of Great Britain is a history of repeated injuries and usurpations, all having in direct object the establishment of an absolute tyranny over these states. To prove this, let facts be submitted to a candid world.

He has refused his assent to laws, the most wholesome and necessary for the public good.

He has forbidden his governors to pass laws of immediate and pressing importance, unless suspended in their operation till his assent should be obtained; and, when so suspended, he has utterly neglected to attend to them.

He has refused to pass other laws for the accommodation of large districts of people, unless those people would relinquish the right of representation in the legislature, a right inestimable to them, and formidable to tyrants only.

He has called together legislative bodies at places unusual, uncomfortable, and distant from the depository of their public records, for the sole purpose of fatiguing them into compliance with his measures.

He has dissolved representative houses repeatedly, for opposing, with manly firmness, his invasions on the rights of the people.

He has refused for a long time, after such dissolutions, to cause others to be elected; whereby the legislative powers, incapable of annihilation, have returned to the people at large for their exercise; the state remaining, in the mean time, exposed to all the dangers of invasions from without and convulsions within.

He has endeavored to prevent the population of these states; for that purpose obstructing the laws for naturalization of foreigners; refusing to pass others to encourage their migration hither, and raising the conditions of new appropriations of lands.

He has obstructed the administration of justice, by refusing his assent to laws for establishing judiciary powers.

He has made judges dependent on his will alone, for the tenure of their offices, and the amount and payment of their salaries.

He has erected a multitude of new offices, and sent hither swarms of officers to harass our people and eat out their substance.

He has kept among us, in times of peace, standing armies, without the consent of our legislatures.

He has affected to render the military independent of, and superior to, the civil power.

He has combined with others to subject us to a jurisdiction foreign to our Constitution and unacknowledged by our laws, giving his assent to their acts of pretended legislation:

For quartering large bodies of armed troops among us;

For protecting them, by a mock trial, from punishment for any murders which they should commit on the inhabitants of these states;

For cutting off our trade with all parts of the world;

For imposing taxes on us without our consent;

For depriving us, in many cases, of the benefits of trial by jury;

For transporting us beyond seas, to be tried for pretended offenses;

For abolishing the free system of English laws in a neighboring province, establishing therein an arbitrary government, and enlarging its boundaries, so as to render it at once an example and fit instrument for introducing the same absolute rule into these colonies;

For taking away our charters, abolishing our most valuable laws, and altering fundamentally the forms of our governments;

For suspending our own legislatures, and declaring themselves invested with power to legislate for us in all cases whatsoever.

He has abdicated government here, by declaring us out of his protection and waging war against us.

He has plundered our seas, ravaged our coasts, burned our towns, and destroyed the lives of our people.

He is at this time transporting large armies of foreign mercenaries to complete the works of death, desolation, and tyranny already begun with circumstances of cruelty and perfidy scarcely par-

alleled in the most barbarous ages, and totally un-
worthy the head of a civilized nation.

He has constrained our fellow-citizens, taken
captive on the high seas, to bear arms against
their country, to become the executioners of their
friends and brethren, or to fall themselves by their
hands.

He has excited domestic insurrection among
us, and has endeavored to bring on the inhabitants of our frontiers the merciless Indian savages,
whose known rule of warfare is an undistinguished
destruction of all ages, sexes, and conditions.

In every stage of these oppressions we have
petitioned for redress in the most humble terms;
our repeated petitions have been answered only
by repeated injury. A prince, whose character is
thus marked by every act which may define a ty-
rant, is unfit to be the ruler of a free people.

Nor have we been wanting in our attentions
to our British brethren. We have warned them,
from time to time, of attempts by their legislature
to extend an unwarrantable jurisdiction over us.
We have reminded them of the circumstances of
our emigration and settlement here. We have ap-
pealed to their native justice and magnanimity;
and we have conjured them, by the ties of our
common kindred, to disavow these usurpations

which would inevitably interrupt our connections and correspondence. They too, have been deaf to the voice of justice and of consanguinity. We must, therefore, acquiesce in the necessity which denounces our separation, and hold them as we hold the rest of mankind, enemies in war, in peace friends.

We, therefore, the *representatives* of the *United States of America*, in General Congress assembled, appealing to the Supreme Judge of the world for the rectitude of our intentions, do, in the name and by the authority of the good people of these colonies solemnly publish and declare, That these United Colonies are, and of right ought to be, *free and independent states*; that they are absolved from all allegiance to the British crown and that all political connection between them and the state of Great Britain is, and ought to be, totally dissolved; and that, as free and independent states, they have full power to levy war, conclude peace, contract alliances, establish commerce, and do all other acts and things which independent states may of right do. And for the support of this declaration, with a firm reliance on the protection of Divine Providence, we mutually pledge to each other our Lives, our Fortunes, and our sacred Honor.

[Signed by]
John Hancock
[President]

Georgia

Button Gwinnett,
Lyman Hall,
George Walton.

South Carolina

Edward Rutledge,
Thomas Hayward, Jr.,
Thomas Lynch, Jr.,
Arthur Middleton.

North Carolina

William Hooper,
Joseph Hewes,
John Penn.

Maryland

Samuel Chase,
William Paca,
Thomas Stone,
Charles Carroll of Carrollton.

Virginia

George Wythe,
Richard Henry Lee,
Thomas Jefferson,
Benjamin Harrison,
Thomas Nelson, Jr.,
Francis Lightfoot Lee,
Carter Braxton.

Pennsylvania

Robert Morris
Benjamin Rush,
Benjamin Franklin,
John Morton,
George Clymer,
James Smith,
George Taylor,
James Wilson,
George Ross.

Delaware

Caesar Rodney,
George Read,
Thomas M'kean.

New York

William Floyd,
Philip Livingston,
Francis Lewis,
Lewis Morris.

New Jersey

Richard Stockton,
John Witherspoon,
Francis Hopkinson,
John Hart,
Abraham Clark.

New Hampshire

Josiah Bartlett,
William Whipple,
Matthew Thornton.

Massachusetts Bay

Samuel Adams,
John Adams,
Robert Treat Paine,
Elbridge Gerry.

Connecticut

Roger Sherman,
Samuel Huntington,
William Williams,
Oliver Wolcott.

Rhode Island

Stephen Hopkins,
William Ellery.

THE CONSTITUTION OF THE UNITED STATES

SEPTEMBER 17, 1787

We the People of the United States, in Order to form a more perfect Union, establish Justice, insure domestic Tranquility, provide for the common defense, promote the general Welfare, and secure the Blessings of Liberty to ourselves and our Posterity, do ordain and establish this Constitution for the United States of America.

Article. I.

SECTION. 1.

All legislative Powers herein granted shall be vested in a Congress of the United States, which shall consist of a Senate and House of Representatives.

SECTION. 2.

The House of Representatives shall be composed of Members chosen every second Year by the People of the several States, and the Electors in each State shall have the Qualifications requisite for Electors of the most numerous Branch of the State Legislature.

No Person shall be a Representative who shall not have attained to the Age of twenty five Years, and been seven Years a Citizen of the United States, and who shall not, when elected, be an Inhabitant of that State in which he shall be chosen.

Representatives and direct Taxes shall be apportioned among the several States which may be included within this Union, according to their respective Numbers, which shall be determined by adding to the whole Number of free Persons, including those bound to Service for a Term of Years, and excluding Indians not taxed, three fifths of all other Persons. The actual Enumeration shall be made within three Years after the first Meeting of the Congress of the United States, and within every subsequent Term of ten Years, in such Manner as they shall by Law direct. The Number of Representatives shall not exceed one for every thirty Thousand, but each State shall have at Least one Representative; and until such enumeration shall be made, the State of New Hampshire shall be entitled to chuse three, Massachusetts eight, Rhode-Island and Providence Plantations one, Connecticut five, New-York six, New Jersey four, Pennsylvania eight, Delaware one, Maryland six, Virginia ten, North Carolina five, South Carolina five, and Georgia three.

When vacancies happen in the Representation from any State, the Executive Authority thereof shall issue Writs of Election to fill such Vacancies.

The House of Representatives shall chuse their Speaker and other Officers; and shall have the sole Power of Impeachment.

SECTION. 3.

The Senate of the United States shall be composed of two Senators from each State, chosen by the Legislature thereof for six Years; and each Senator shall have one Vote.

Immediately after they shall be assembled in Consequence of the first Election, they shall be divided as equally as may be into three Classes. The Seats of the Senators of the first Class shall be vacated at the Expiration of the second Year, of the second Class at the Expiration of the fourth Year, and of the third Class at the Expiration of the sixth Year, so that one third may be chosen every second Year; and if Vacancies happen by Resignation, or otherwise, during the Recess of the Legislature of any State, the Executive thereof may make temporary Appointments until the next Meeting of the Legislature, which shall then fill such Vacancies.

No Person shall be a Senator who shall not have attained to the Age of thirty Years, and been nine Years a Citizen of the United States, and who shall not, when elected, be an Inhabitant of that State for which he shall be chosen.

The Vice President of the United States shall be President of the Senate, but shall have no Vote, unless they be equally divided.

The Senate shall chuse their other Officers, and also a President pro tempore, in the Absence of the Vice President, or when he shall exercise the Office of President of the United States.

The Senate shall have the sole Power to try all Impeachments. When sitting for that Purpose, they shall be on Oath or Affirmation. When the President of the United States is tried, the Chief Justice shall preside: And no Person shall be convicted without the Concurrence of two thirds of the Members present.

Judgment in Cases of Impeachment shall not extend further than to removal from Office, and disqualification to hold and enjoy any Office of honor, Trust or Profit under the United States: but the Party convicted shall nevertheless be liable and subject to Indictment, Trial, Judgment and Punishment, according to Law.

SECTION. 4.

The Times, Places and Manner of holding Elections for Senators and Representatives, shall be prescribed in each State by the Legislature thereof; but the Congress may at any time by Law make or alter such Regulations, except as to the Places of chusing Senators.

The Congress shall assemble at least once in every Year, and such Meeting shall be on the first Monday in December, unless they shall by Law appoint a different Day.

SECTION. 5.

Each House shall be the Judge of the Elections, Returns and Qualifications of its own Members, and a Majority of each shall constitute a Quorum to do Business; but a smaller Number may adjourn from day to day, and may be authorized to compel the Attendance of absent Members, in such Manner, and under such Penalties as each House may provide.

Each House may determine the Rules of its Proceedings, punish its Members for disorderly Behaviour, and, with the Concurrence of two thirds, expel a Member.

Each House shall keep a Journal of its Proceedings, and from time to time publish the same, excepting such Parts as may in their Judgment require Secrecy; and the Yeas and Nays of the Members of either House on any question shall, at the Desire of one fifth of those Present, be entered on the Journal.

Neither House, during the Session of Congress, shall, without the Consent of the other, adjourn for more than three days, nor to any other Place than that in which the two Houses shall be sitting.

SECTION. 6.

The Senators and Representatives shall receive a Compensation for their Services, to be ascertained by Law, and paid out of the Treasury of the United States. They shall in all Cases, except Treason, Felony and Breach of the Peace, be privileged from Arrest during their Attendance at the Session of their respective Houses, and in going to and returning from the same; and for any Speech or Debate in either House, they shall not be questioned in any other Place.

No Senator or Representative shall, during the Time for which he was elected, be appointed to any civil Office under the Authority of the United States, which shall have been created, or the

Emoluments whereof shall have been encreased during such time; and no Person holding any Office under the United States, shall be a Member of either House during his Continuance in Office.

SECTION. 7.

All Bills for raising Revenue shall originate in the House of Representatives; but the Senate may propose or concur with Amendments as on other Bills.

Every Bill which shall have passed the House of Representatives and the Senate, shall, before it become a Law, be presented to the President of the United States: If he approve he shall sign it, but if not he shall return it, with his Objections to that House in which it shall have originated, who shall enter the Objections at large on their Journal, and proceed to reconsider it. If after such Reconsideration two thirds of that House shall agree to pass the Bill, it shall be sent, together with the Objections, to the other House, by which it shall likewise be reconsidered, and if approved by two thirds of that House, it shall become a Law. But in all such Cases the Votes of both Houses shall be determined by yeas and Nays, and the Names of the Persons voting for and against the Bill shall be entered on the Journal of each House respectively. If any Bill shall not be returned by the President within ten Days (Sundays excepted) after it shall have been presented to him, the Same shall be a Law, in like Manner as if he had signed it, unless the Congress by their Adjournment prevent its Return, in which Case it shall not be a Law.

Every Order, Resolution, or Vote to which the Concurrence of the Senate and House of Representatives may be necessary (except on a question of Adjournment) shall be presented to the President of the United States; and before the Same shall take Effect, shall be approved by him, or being disapproved by him, shall be repassed by two thirds of the Senate and House of Representatives, according to the Rules and Limitations prescribed in the Case of a Bill.

SECTION. 8.

The Congress shall have Power To lay and collect Taxes, Duties, Imposts and Excises, to pay the Debts and provide for the common Defence and general Welfare of the United States; but all Duties, Imposts and Excises shall be uniform throughout the United States;

To borrow Money on the credit of the United States;

To regulate Commerce with foreign Nations,

and among the several States, and with the Indian Tribes;

To establish an uniform Rule of Naturalization, and uniform Laws on the subject of Bankruptcies throughout the United States;

To coin Money, regulate the Value thereof, and of foreign Coin, and fix the Standard of Weights and Measures;

To provide for the Punishment of counterfeiting the Securities and current Coin of the United States;

To establish Post Offices and post Roads;

To promote the Progress of Science and useful Arts, by securing for limited Times to Authors and Inventors the exclusive Right to their respective Writings and Discoveries;

To constitute Tribunals inferior to the supreme Court;

To define and punish Piracies and Felonies committed on the high Seas, and Offences against the Law of Nations;

To declare War, grant Letters of Marque and Reprisal, and make Rules concerning Captures on Land and Water;

To raise and support Armies, but no Appropriation of Money to that Use shall be for a longer Term than two Years;

To provide and maintain a Navy;

To make Rules for the Government and Regulation of the land and naval Forces;

To provide for calling forth the Militia to execute the Laws of the Union, suppress Insurrections and repel Invasions;

To provide for organizing, arming, and disciplining, the Militia, and for governing such Part of them as may be employed in the Service of the United States, reserving to the States respectively, the Appointment of the Officers, and the Authority of training the Militia according to the discipline prescribed by Congress;

To exercise exclusive Legislation in all Cases whatsoever, over such District (not exceeding ten Miles square) as may, by Cession of particular States, and the Acceptance of Congress, become the Seat of the Government of the United States, and to exercise like Authority over all Places purchased by the Consent of the Legislature of the State in which the Same shall be, for the Erection of Forts, Magazines, Arsenals, dock-Yards, and other needful Buildings;—And

To make all Laws which shall be necessary and proper for carrying into Execution the foregoing Powers, and all other Powers vested by this Constitution in the Government of the United States, or in any Department or Officer thereof.

SECTION. 9.

The Migration or Importation of such Persons as any of the States now existing shall think proper to admit, shall not be prohibited by the Congress prior to the Year one thousand eight hundred and eight, but a Tax or duty may be imposed on such Importation, not exceeding ten dollars for each Person.

The Privilege of the Writ of Habeas Corpus shall not be suspended, unless when in Cases of Rebellion or Invasion the public Safety may require it.

No Bill of Attainder or ex post facto Law shall be passed.

No Capitation, or other direct, Tax shall be laid, unless in Proportion to the Census or enumeration herein before directed to be taken.

No Tax or Duty shall be laid on Articles exported from any State.

No Preference shall be given by any Regulation of Commerce or Revenue to the Ports of one State over those of another; nor shall Vessels bound to, or from, one State, be obliged to enter, clear, or pay Duties in another.

No Money shall be drawn from the Treasury, but in Consequence of Appropriations made by Law; and a regular Statement and Account of the Receipts and Expenditures of all public Money shall be published from time to time.

No Title of Nobility shall be granted by the United States: And no Person holding any Office of Profit or Trust under them, shall, without the Consent of the Congress, accept of any present, Emolument, Office, or Title, of any kind whatever, from any King, Prince, or foreign State.

SECTION. 10.

No State shall enter into any Treaty, Alliance, or Confederation; grant Letters of Marque and Reprisal; coin Money; emit Bills of Credit; make any Thing but gold and silver Coin a Tender in Payment of Debts; pass any Bill of Attainder, ex post facto Law, or Law impairing the Obligation of Contracts, or grant any Title of Nobility.

No State shall, without the Consent of the Congress, lay any Imposts or Duties on Imports or Exports, except what may be absolutely necessary for executing it's inspection Laws: and the net Produce of all Duties and Imposts, laid by any State on Imports or Exports, shall be for the Use of the Treasury of the United States; and all such Laws shall be subject to the Revision and Controul of the Congress.

No State shall, without the Consent of Congress, lay any Duty of Tonnage, keep Troops, or Ships of War in time of Peace, enter into any Agreement or Compact with another State, or with a foreign Power, or engage in War, unless actually invaded, or in such imminent Danger as will not admit of delay.

Article. II.

SECTION. 1.

The executive Power shall be vested in a President of the United States of America. He shall hold his Office during the Term of four Years, and, together with the Vice President, chosen for the same Term, be elected, as follows:

Each State shall appoint, in such Manner as the Legislature thereof may direct, a Number of Electors, equal to the whole Number of Senators and Representatives to which the State may be entitled in the Congress: but no Senator or Representative, or Person holding an Office of Trust or Profit under the United States, shall be appointed an Elector.

The Electors shall meet in their respective States, and vote by Ballot for two Persons, of whom one at least shall not be an Inhabitant of the same State with themselves. And they shall make a List of all the Persons voted for, and of the Number of Votes for each; which List they shall sign and certify, and transmit sealed to the Seat of the Government of the United States, directed to the President of the Senate. The President of the Senate shall, in the Presence of the Senate and House of Representatives, open all the Certificates, and the Votes shall then be counted. The Person having the greatest Number of Votes shall be the President, if such Number be a Majority of the whole Number of Electors appointed; and if there be more than one who have such Majority, and have an equal Number of Votes, then the House of Representatives shall immediately chuse by Ballot one of them for President; and if no Person have a Majority, then from the five highest on the List the said House shall in like Manner chuse the President. But in chusing the President, the Votes shall be taken by States, the Representation from each State having one Vote; A quorum for this purpose shall consist of a Member or Members from two thirds of the States, and a Majority of all the States shall be necessary to a Choice. In every Case, after the Choice of the President, the Person having the greatest Number of Votes of the Electors shall be the Vice President. But if there should remain two or more who have equal Votes, the Senate shall chuse from them by Ballot the Vice President.

The Congress may determine the Time of chusing the Electors, and the Day on which they shall give their Votes; which Day shall be the same throughout the United States.

No Person except a natural born Citizen, or a Citizen of the United States, at the time of the Adoption of this Constitution, shall be eligible to the Office of President; neither shall any Person be eligible to that Office who shall not have attained to the Age of thirty five Years, and been fourteen Years a Resident within the United States.

In Case of the Removal of the President from Office, or of his Death, Resignation, or Inability to discharge the Powers and Duties of the said Office, the Same shall devolve on the Vice President, and the Congress may by Law provide for the Case of Removal, Death, Resignation or Inability, both of the President and Vice President, declaring what Officer shall then act as President, and such Officer shall act accordingly, until the Disability be removed, or a President shall be elected.

The President shall, at stated Times, receive for his Services, a Compensation, which shall neither be increased nor diminished during the Period for which he shall have been elected, and he shall not receive within that Period any other Emolument from the United States, or any of them.

Before he enter on the Execution of his Office, he shall take the following Oath or Affirmation:—
"I do solemnly swear (or affirm) that I will faithfully execute the Office of President of the United States, and will to the best of my Ability, preserve, protect and defend the Constitution of the United States."

SECTION. 2.

The President shall be Commander in Chief of the Army and Navy of the United States, and of the Militia of the several States, when called into the actual Service of the United States; he may require the Opinion, in writing, of the principal Officer in each of the executive Departments, upon any Subject relating to the Duties of their respective Offices, and he shall have Power to grant Reprieves and Pardons for Offences against the United States, except in Cases of Impeachment.

He shall have Power, by and with the Advice and Consent of the Senate, to make Treaties, provided two thirds of the Senators present concur; and he shall nominate, and by and with the Advice and Consent of the Senate, shall appoint Ambassadors, other public Ministers and Consuls, Judges of the supreme Court, and all other Officers of the United States, whose Appointments are not herein otherwise provided for, and which shall be established by Law: but the Congress may by Law vest the Appointment of such inferior Officers, as they think proper, in the President alone, in the Courts of Law, or in the Heads of Departments.

The President shall have Power to fill up all Vacancies that may happen during the Recess of the Senate, by granting Commissions which shall expire at the End of their next Session.

SECTION. 3.

He shall from time to time give to the Congress Information of the State of the Union, and recommend to their Consideration such Measures as he shall judge necessary and expedient; he may, on extraordinary Occasions, convene both Houses, or either of them, and in Case of Disagreement between them, with Respect to the Time of Adjournment, he may adjourn them to such Time as he shall think proper; he shall receive Ambassadors and other public Ministers; he shall take Care that the Laws be faithfully executed, and shall Commission all the Officers of the United States.

SECTION. 4.

The President, Vice President and all civil Officers of the United States, shall be removed from Office on Impeachment for, and Conviction of, Treason, Bribery, or other high Crimes and Misdemeanors.

Article III.

SECTION. 1.

The judicial Power of the United States shall be vested in one supreme Court, and in such inferior Courts as the Congress may from time to time ordain and establish. The Judges, both of the supreme and inferior Courts, shall hold their Offices during good Behaviour, and shall, at stated Times, receive for their Services a Compensation, which shall not be diminished during their Continuance in Office.

SECTION. 2.

The judicial Power shall extend to all Cases, in Law and Equity, arising under this Constitution, the Laws of the United States, and Treaties made, or which shall be made, under their Authority;—to all Cases affecting Ambassadors, other public Ministers and Consuls;—to all Cases of admiralty and maritime Jurisdiction;—to Controversies to which the United States shall be a Party;—to Controversies between two or more States;—between a State and Citizens of another State,—between Citizens of different States,—between Citizens of the same State claiming Lands under Grants of different States, and between a State, or the Citizens thereof, and foreign States, Citizens or Subjects.

In all Cases affecting Ambassadors, other public Ministers and Consuls, and those in which a State shall be Party, the supreme Court shall have original Jurisdiction. In all the other Cases before mentioned, the supreme Court shall have appellate Jurisdiction, both as to Law and Fact, with such Exceptions, and under such Regulations as the Congress shall make.

The Trial of all Crimes, except in Cases of Impeachment, shall be by Jury; and such Trial shall be held in the State where the said Crimes shall have been committed; but when not committed within any State, the Trial shall be at such Place or Places as the Congress may by Law have directed.

SECTION. 3.

Treason against the United States, shall consist only in levying War against them, or in adhering to their Enemies, giving them Aid and Comfort. No Person shall be convicted of Treason unless on the Testimony of two Witnesses to the same overt Act, or on Confession in open Court.

The Congress shall have Power to declare the Punishment of Treason, but no Attainder of Treason shall work Corruption of Blood, or Forfeiture except during the Life of the Person attainted.

Article. IV.

SECTION. 1.

Full Faith and Credit shall be given in each State to the public Acts, Records, and judicial Proceedings of every other State. And the Congress may by general Laws prescribe the Manner in which such Acts, Records and Proceedings shall be proved, and the Effect thereof.

SECTION. 2.

The Citizens of each State shall be entitled to all Privileges and Immunities of Citizens in the several States.

A Person charged in any State with Treason, Felony, or other Crime, who shall flee from Justice, and be found in another State, shall on Demand of the executive Authority of the State from which he fled, be delivered up, to be removed to the State having Jurisdiction of the Crime.

No Person held to Service or Labour in one State, under the Laws thereof, escaping into another, shall, in Consequence of any Law or Regulation therein, be discharged from such Service or Labour, but shall be delivered up on Claim of the Party to whom such Service or Labour may be due.

SECTION. 3.

New States may be admitted by the Congress into this Union; but no new State shall be formed or erected within the Jurisdiction of any other State; nor any State be formed by the Junction of two or more States, or Parts of States, without the Consent of the Legislatures of the States concerned as well as of the Congress.

The Congress shall have Power to dispose of

and make all needful Rules and Regulations respecting the Territory or other Property belonging to the United States; and nothing in this Constitution shall be so construed as to Prejudice any Claims of the United States, or of any particular State.

SECTION. 4.

The United States shall guarantee to every State in this Union a Republican Form of Government, and shall protect each of them against Invasion; and on Application of the Legislature, or of the Executive (when the Legislature cannot be convened), against domestic Violence.

Article. V.

The Congress, whenever two thirds of both Houses shall deem it necessary, shall propose Amendments to this Constitution, or, on the Application of the Legislatures of two thirds of the several States, shall call a Convention for proposing Amendments, which, in either Case, shall be valid to all Intents and Purposes, as Part of this Constitution, when ratified by the Legislatures of three fourths of the several States, or by Conventions in three fourths thereof, as the one or the other Mode of Ratification may be proposed by the Congress; Provided that no Amendment which may be made prior to the Year One thousand eight hundred and eight shall in any Manner affect the first and fourth Clauses in the Ninth Section of the first Article; and that no State, without its Consent, shall be deprived of its equal Suffrage in the Senate.

Article. VI.

All Debts contracted and Engagements entered into, before the Adoption of this Constitution, shall be as valid against the United States under this Constitution, as under the Confederation.

This Constitution, and the Laws of the United States which shall be made in Pursuance thereof; and all Treaties made, or which shall be made, under the Authority of the United States, shall be the supreme Law of the Land; and the Judges in every State shall be bound thereby, any Thing in the Constitution or Laws of any State to the Contrary notwithstanding.

The Senators and Representatives before mentioned, and the Members of the several State Legislatures, and all executive and judicial Officers, both of the United States and of the several

States, shall be bound by Oath or Affirmation, to support this Constitution; but no religious Test shall ever be required as a Qualification to any Office or public Trust under the United States.

Article. VII.

The Ratification of the Conventions of nine States, shall be sufficient for the Establishment of this Constitution between the States so ratifying the Same.

The Word, "the," being interlined between the seventh and eighth Lines of the first Page, the Word "Thirty" being partly written on an Erazure in the fifteenth Line of the first Page, The Words "is tried" being interlined between the thirty second and thirty third Lines of the first Page and the Word "the" being interlined between the forty third and forty fourth Lines of the second Page.

Attest William Jackson Secretary

Done in Convention by the Unanimous Consent of the States present the Seventeenth Day of September in the Year of our Lord one thousand seven hundred and Eighty seven and of the Indepen-

dence of the United States of America the Twelfth
In witness whereof We have hereunto sub-
scribed our Names,

George Washington
President and deputy from Virginia

Delaware

George Read
Gunning Bedford jun
John Dickinson
Richard Bassett
Jacob Broom

Maryland

James McHenry
Daniel of St Thomas Jenifer
Daniel Carroll

Virginia

John Blair
James Madison, Jr.

North Carolina

William Blount
Richard Dobbs Spaight
Hugh Williamson

South Carolina

John Rutledge
Charles Cotesworth Pinckney
Charles Pinckney
Pierce Butler

Georgia

William Few
Abraham Baldwin

New Hampshire

John Langdon
Nicholas Gilman

Massachusetts

Nathaniel Gorham
Rufus King

Connecticut

William Samuel Johnson
Roger Sherman

New York

Alexander Hamilton

New Jersey

William Livingston
David Brearley
William Paterson
Jonathan Dayton

Pennsylvania

Benjamin Franklin
Thomas Mifflin
Robert Morris
George Clymer
Thomas FitzSimons
Jared Ingersoll
James Wilson
Gouverneur Morris

THE AMENDMENTS
TO THE
CONSTITUTION
OF THE
UNITED STATES

The Bill of Rights

Note: The first ten amendments to the Constitution were ratified December 15, 1791, and form what is known as the "Bill of Rights." These amendments were transcribed in their original form. The capitalization and punctuation in this version is from the enrolled original of the 1789 Joint Resolution of Congress proposing the Bill of Rights.

Amendment I

Congress shall make no law respecting an establishment of religion, or prohibiting the free exercise thereof; or abridging the freedom of speech, or of the press; or the right of the people peaceably to assemble, and to petition the Government for a redress of grievances.

Amendment II

A well regulated Militia, being necessary to the security of a free State, the right of the people to keep and bear Arms, shall not be infringed.

Amendment III

No Soldier shall, in time of peace be quartered in any house, without the consent of the Owner, nor in time of war, but in a manner to be prescribed by law.

Amendment IV

The right of the people to be secure in their persons, houses, papers, and effects, against unreasonable searches and seizures, shall not be violated, and no Warrants shall issue, but upon probable cause, supported by Oath or affirmation, and particularly describing the place to be searched, and the persons or things to be seized.

Amendment V

No person shall be held to answer for a capital, or otherwise infamous crime, unless on a present-ment or indictment of a Grand Jury, except in cases arising in the land or naval forces, or in the Militia, when in actual service in time of War or public danger; nor shall any person be subject for the same offence to be twice put in jeopardy of life or limb; nor shall be compelled in any criminal case to be a witness against himself, nor be de-prived of life, liberty, or property, without due pro-cess of law; nor shall private property be taken for public use, without just compensation.

Amendment VI

In all criminal prosecutions, the accused shall en-joy the right to a speedy and public trial, by an impartial jury of the State and district wherein the crime shall have been committed, which district shall have been previously ascertained by law, and to be informed of the nature and cause of the accusation; to be confronted with the witnesses against him; to have compulsory process for obtaining witnesses in his favor, and to have the Assistance of Counsel for his defence.

Amendment VII

In Suits at common law, where the value in controversy shall exceed twenty dollars, the right of trial by jury shall be preserved, and no fact tried by a jury, shall be otherwise re-examined in any Court of the United States, than according to the rules of the common law.

Amendment VIII

Excessive bail shall not be required, nor excessive fines imposed, nor cruel and unusual punishments inflicted.

Amendment IX

The enumeration in the Constitution, of certain rights, shall not be construed to deny or disparage others retained by the people.

Amendment X

The powers not delegated to the United States by the Constitution, nor prohibited by it to the States, are reserved to the States respectively, or to the people.

Amendment XI

Passed by Congress March 4, 1794.
Ratified February 7, 1795.

Note: Article III, section 2, of the Constitution was modified by the 11th amendment.

The Judicial power of the United States shall not be construed to extend to any suit in law or equity, commenced or prosecuted against one of the United States by Citizens of another State, or by Citizens or Subjects of any Foreign State.

Amendment XII

Passed by Congress December 9, 1803.
Ratified June 15, 1804.

Note: A portion of Article II, section 1 of the Constitution was superseded by the 12th amendment.

The Electors shall meet in their respective states and vote by ballot for President and Vice-President, one of whom, at least, shall not be an inhabitant of the same state with themselves; they shall name in their ballots the person voted for as President, and in distinct ballots the person voted for as Vice-President, and they shall make distinct lists of all persons voted for as President, and of all persons voted for as Vice-President, and of the number of votes for each, which lists they shall sign and certify, and transmit sealed to the seat of the government of the United States, directed to the President of the Senate; — the President of the Senate shall, in the presence of the Senate and House of Representatives, open all the certificates and the votes shall then be counted; — The person having the greatest number of votes for President, shall be the President, if such number be a majority of the whole number of Electors appointed; and if no person have such majority, then from the persons having the highest numbers not exceeding three on the list of those voted for as President, the House of Representatives shall choose immediately, by ballot, the President. But in choosing the President, the votes shall be taken by states, the representation from each state having one vote; a quorum for this purpose shall consist of a member or members from two-thirds of the states, and a majority of all the states shall be necessary to a choice. [And if the House of Representatives shall not choose a President whenever the right of choice shall devolve upon them, before the fourth day of March next following, then the Vice-President shall act as President, as in case of the death or other constitutional disability of the President. —][1] The person having the greatest number of votes as Vice-President, shall be the Vice-President, if such number be a majority of the whole number of Electors appointed, and if no person have a majority, then from the two highest numbers on the list, the Senate shall choose the Vice-President; a quorum for the purpose shall consist of two-thirds of the

---

1. Superseded by section 3 of the 20th amendment.

whole number of Senators, and a majority of the whole number shall be necessary to a choice. But no person constitutionally ineligible to the office of President shall be eligible to that of Vice-President of the United States.

Amendment XIII

Passed by Congress January 31, 1865.
Ratified December 6, 1865.

Note: A portion of Article IV, section 2, of the Constitution was superseded by the 13th amendment.

SECTION 1.

Neither slavery nor involuntary servitude, except as a punishment for crime whereof the party shall have been duly convicted, shall exist within the United States, or any place subject to their jurisdiction.

SECTION 2.

Congress shall have power to enforce this article by appropriate legislation.

Amendment XIV

Passed by Congress June 13, 1866.
Ratified July 9, 1868.

Note: Article I, section 2, of the Constitution was modified by section 2 of the 14th amendment.

SECTION 1.

All persons born or naturalized in the United States, and subject to the jurisdiction thereof, are citizens of the United States and of the State wherein they reside. No State shall make or enforce any law which shall abridge the privileges or immunities of citizens of the United States; nor shall any State deprive any person of life, liberty, or property, without due process of law; nor deny to any person within its jurisdiction the equal protection of the laws.

SECTION 2.

Representatives shall be apportioned among the several States according to their respective numbers, counting the whole number of persons in each State, excluding Indians not taxed. But when the right to vote at any election for the choice of electors for President and Vice-President of the United States, Representatives in Congress, the Executive and Judicial officers of a State, or the members of the Legislature thereof, is denied to any of the male inhabitants of such State, being twenty-one years of age,[2] and citizens of the United States, or in any way abridged, except for participation in rebellion, or other crime, the basis of representation therein shall be reduced in the proportion which the number of such male citizens shall bear to the whole number of male citizens twenty-one years of age in such State.

SECTION 3.

No person shall be a Senator or Representative in Congress, or elector of President and Vice-President, or hold any office, civil or military, under the United States, or under any State, who, having previously taken an oath, as a member of Congress, or as an officer of the United States, or as a member of any State legislature, or as an executive or judicial officer of any State, to support the Constitution of the United States, shall have engaged in insurrection or rebellion against the

2. Changed by section 1 of the 26th amendment.

same, or given aid or comfort to the enemies thereof. But Congress may by a vote of two-thirds of each House, remove such disability.

SECTION 4.

The validity of the public debt of the United States, authorized by law, including debts incurred for payment of pensions and bounties for services in suppressing insurrection or rebellion, shall not be questioned. But neither the United States nor any State shall assume or pay any debt or obligation incurred in aid of insurrection or rebellion against the United States, or any claim for the loss or emancipation of any slave; but all such debts, obligations and claims shall be held illegal and void.

SECTION 5.

The Congress shall have the power to enforce, by appropriate legislation, the provisions of this article.

Amendment XV

Passed by Congress February 26, 1869.
Ratified February 3, 1870.

SECTION 1.

The right of citizens of the United States to vote shall not be denied or abridged by the United States or by any State on account of race, color, or previous condition of servitude—

SECTION 2.

The Congress shall have the power to enforce this article by appropriate legislation.

Amendment XVI

Passed by Congress July 2, 1909.
Ratified February 3, 1913.

Note: Article I, section 9, of the Constitution was modified by the 16th amendment.

The Congress shall have power to lay and collect taxes on incomes, from whatever source derived, without apportionment among the several States, and without regard to any census or enumeration.

Amendment XVII

**Passed by Congress May 13, 1912.
Ratified April 8, 1913.**

Note: Article I, section 3, of the Constitution was modified by the 17th amendment.

The Senate of the United States shall be composed of two Senators from each State, elected by the people thereof, for six years; and each Senator shall have one vote. The electors in each State shall have the qualifications requisite for electors of the most numerous branch of the State legislatures.

When vacancies happen in the representation of any State in the Senate, the executive authority of such State shall issue writs of election to fill such vacancies: *Provided*, That the legislature of any State may empower the executive thereof to make temporary appointments until the people fill the vacancies by election as the legislature may direct.

This amendment shall not be so construed as to affect the election or term of any Senator chosen before it becomes valid as part of the Constitution.

Amendment XVIII

Passed by Congress December 18, 1917.
Ratified January 16, 1919.
Repealed by the 21st amendment.

SECTION 1.

After one year from the ratification of this article the manufacture, sale, or transportation of intoxicating liquors within, the importation thereof into, or the exportation thereof from the United States and all territory subject to the jurisdiction thereof for beverage purposes is hereby prohibited.

SECTION 2.

The Congress and the several States shall have concurrent power to enforce this article by appropriate legislation.

SECTION 3.

This article shall be inoperative unless it shall have been ratified as an amendment to the Constitution by the legislatures of the several States, as provided in the Constitution, within seven years from the date of the submission hereof to the States by the Congress.

Amendment XIX

Passed by Congress June 4, 1919.
Ratified August 18, 1920.

The right of citizens of the United States to vote shall not be denied or abridged by the United States or by any State on account of sex.

Congress shall have power to enforce this article by appropriate legislation.

Amendment XX

Passed by Congress March 2, 1932.
Ratified January 23, 1933.

Note: Article I, section 4, of the Constitution was modified by section 2 of this amendment. In addition, a portion of the 12th amendment was superseded by section 3.

SECTION 1.

The terms of the President and the Vice President shall end at noon on the 20th day of January, and the terms of Senators and Representatives at noon on the 3d day of January, of the years in which such terms would have ended if this article had not been ratified; and the terms of their successors shall then begin.

SECTION 2.

The Congress shall assemble at least once in every year, and such meeting shall begin at noon on the 3d day of January, unless they shall by law appoint a different day.

SECTION 3.

If, at the time fixed for the beginning of the term of the President, the President elect shall have died, the Vice President elect shall become President. If a President shall not have been chosen before the time fixed for the beginning of his term, or if the President elect shall have failed to qualify, then the Vice President elect shall act as President until a President shall have qualified; and the Congress may by law provide for the case wherein neither a President elect nor a Vice President elect shall have qualified, declaring who shall then act as President, or the manner in which one who is to act shall be selected, and such person shall act accordingly until a President or Vice President shall have qualified.

SECTION 4.

The Congress may by law provide for the case of the death of any of the persons from whom the House of Representatives may choose a President whenever the right of choice shall have devolved upon them, and for the case of the death of any of the persons from whom the Senate may choose a Vice President whenever the right of choice shall have devolved upon them.

SECTION 5.

Sections 1 and 2 shall take effect on the 15th day of October following the ratification of this article.

SECTION 6.

This article shall be inoperative unless it shall have been ratified as an amendment to the Constitution by the legislatures of three-fourths of the several States within seven years from the date of its submission.

Amendment XXI

Passed by Congress February 20, 1933.
Ratified December 5, 1933.

SECTION 1.

The eighteenth article of amendment to the Constitution of the United States is hereby repealed.

SECTION 2.

The transportation or importation into any State, Territory, or possession of the United States for delivery or use therein of intoxicating liquors, in violation of the laws thereof, is hereby prohibited.

SECTION 3.

This article shall be inoperative unless it shall have been ratified as an amendment to the Constitution by conventions in the several States, as provided in the Constitution, within seven years from the date of the submission hereof to the States by the Congress.

Amendment XXII

Passed by Congress March 21, 1947.
Ratified February 27, 1951.

SECTION 1.

No person shall be elected to the office of the President more than twice, and no person who has held the office of President, or acted as President, for more than two years of a term to which some other person was elected President shall be elected to the office of the President more than once. But this Article shall not apply to any person holding the office of President when this Article was proposed by the Congress, and shall not prevent any person who may be holding the office of President, or acting as President, during the term within which this Article becomes operative from holding the office of President or acting as President during the remainder of such term.

SECTION 2.

This article shall be inoperative unless it shall have been ratified as an amendment to the Constitution by the legislatures of three-fourths of the several States within seven years from the date of its submission to the States by the Congress.

Amendment XXIII

Passed by Congress June 16, 1960.
Ratified March 29, 1961.

SECTION 1.

The District constituting the seat of Government of the United States shall appoint in such manner as the Congress may direct:

A number of electors of President and Vice President equal to the whole number of Senators and Representatives in Congress to which the District would be entitled if it were a State, but in no event more than the least populous State; they shall be in addition to those appointed by the States, but they shall be considered, for the purposes of the election of President and Vice President, to be electors appointed by a State; and they shall meet in the District and perform such duties as provided by the twelfth article of amendment.

SECTION 2.

The Congress shall have power to enforce this article by appropriate legislation.

Amendment XXIV

Passed by Congress August 27, 1962.
Ratified January 23, 1964.

SECTION 1.

The right of citizens of the United States to vote in any primary or other election for President or Vice President, for electors for President or Vice President, or for Senator or Representative in Congress, shall not be denied or abridged by the United States or any State by reason of failure to pay any poll tax or other tax.

SECTION 2.

The Congress shall have power to enforce this article by appropriate legislation.

Amendment XXV

Passed by Congress July 6, 1965.
Ratified February 10, 1967.

Note: Article II, section 1, of the Constitution was affected by the 25th amendment.

SECTION 1.

In case of the removal of the President from office or of his death or resignation, the Vice President shall become President.

SECTION 2.

Whenever there is a vacancy in the office of the Vice President, the President shall nominate a Vice President who shall take office upon confirmation by a majority vote of both Houses of Congress.

SECTION 3.

Whenever the President transmits to the President pro tempore of the Senate and the Speaker of the House of Representatives his written declaration that he is unable to discharge the powers and duties of his office, and until he transmits to them a written declaration to the contrary, such powers and duties shall be discharged by the Vice President as Acting President.

SECTION 4.

Whenever the Vice President and a majority of either the principal officers of the executive departments or of such other body as Congress may by law provide, transmit to the President pro tempore of the Senate and the Speaker of the House of Representatives their written declaration that the President is unable to discharge the powers and duties of his office, the Vice President shall immediately assume the powers and duties of the office as Acting President.

Thereafter, when the President transmits to the President pro tempore of the Senate and the Speaker of the House of Representatives his written declaration that no inability exists, he shall resume the powers and duties of his office unless the Vice President and a majority of either the principal officers of the executive department or of such other body as Congress may by law provide, transmit within four days to the President pro tempore of the Senate and the Speaker of the House of Representatives their written declaration that the President is unable to discharge the powers and duties of his office. Thereupon Congress shall decide the issue, assembling within forty-eight hours for that purpose if not in session. If the Congress, within twenty-one days after receipt of the latter written declaration, or, if Congress is not in session, within twenty-one days after Congress is required to assemble, determines by two-thirds vote of both Houses that the President is unable to discharge the powers and duties of his office, the Vice President shall continue to discharge the same as Acting President; otherwise, the President shall resume the powers and duties of his office.

Amendment XXVI

Passed by Congress March 23, 1971.
Ratified July 1, 1971.

Note: Amendment 14, section 2, of the Constitution was modified by section 1 of the 26th amendment.

SECTION 1.

The right of citizens of the United States, who are eighteen years of age or older, to vote shall not be denied or abridged by the United States or by any State on account of age.

SECTION 2.

The Congress shall have power to enforce this article by appropriate legislation.

Amendment XXVII

**Originally proposed Sept. 25, 1789.
Ratified May 7, 1992.**

Note: The 27th amendment was initially ratified by six states (Maryland, North Carolina, South Carolina, Delaware, Vermont, and Virginia), and the other eight states excluded, omitted, rejected, or excepted it. It was ratified by various states over time, and in 1992 was fully ratified as an amendment to the Constitution.

No law, varying the compensation for the services of the Senators and Representatives, shall take effect, until an election of Representatives shall have intervened.

INDEX

TO THE

CONSTITUTION

AND THE

AMENDMENTS

Note: Articles noted are of original Constitution or of amendment.

	Article	Section	Clause
To support the Constitution. Senators and Representatives, members of State legislatures, executive and judicial officers, both State and Federal, shall be bound by oath or	6	—	3
Age. No person shall be a Representative who shall not have attained twenty-five years of	1	2	2
No person shall be a Senator who shall not have attained thirty years of	1	3	3
Right of citizens of the United States, who are eighteen years of age or older, to vote shall not be denied or abridged by the United States or any State on account of age. [Amendments]	26	1	—
Agreement or compact with another State without the consent of Congress. No State shall enter into any	1	10	3
Aid and comfort. Treason against the United States shall consist in levying war against them, adhering to their enemies, and giving them	3	3	1
Alliance or confederation. No State shall enter into any treaty of	1	10	1
Ambassadors, or other public ministers and consuls. The President may appoint	2	2	2
The judicial power of the United States shall extend to all cases affecting	3	2	1
Amendments to the Constitution. Whenever two-thirds of both Houses shall deem it necessary, Congress shall propose	5	—	—
On application of the legislatures of two-thirds of the States, Congress shall call a convention to propose	5	—	—
Shall be valid when ratified by the legislatures of, or by conventions in, three-fourths of the States...	5	—	—

	Article	Section	Clause
Appropriate legislation. Congress shall have power to make all laws necessary and proper for carrying into execution the foregoing powers, and all other powers vested by the Constitution in the Government of the United States, or on any department or officer thereof...............	1	8	18
Congress shall have power to enforce the thirteenth article, prohibiting slavery by. [Amendments]..	13	2	—
Congress shall have power to enforce the provisions of the fourteenth article by. [Amendments]..	14	5	—
Congress shall have power to enforce the provisions of the fifteenth article by. [Amendments]..	15	2	—
Congress and the several States shall have concurrent power to enforce the provisions of the eighteenth article. [Amendments] ...	18	2	—
Congress shall have power to enforce the provisions of the nineteenth article. [Amendments]..	19	—	—
Congress shall have power to enforce the provisions of the twenty-third article by. [Amendments]..	23	2	—
Congress shall have power to enforce the provisions of the twenty-fourth article by. [Amendments]..	24	2	—
Congress shall have power to enforce the provisions of the twenty-sixth article by. [Amendments]..	26	2	—
Appropriation of money for raising and supporting armies shall be for a longer term than two years. But no.................................	1	8	12
Appropriations made by law. No money shall be drawn from the Treasury but in consequence of	1	9	7
Approve and sign a bill before it shall become a law. The President shall	1	7	2

	Article	Section	Clause
Attainder, ex post facto law, or law impairing the obligation of contracts. No State shall pass any bill of	1	10	1
Authors and inventors the exclusive right to their writings and inventions. Congress shall have power to secure to..........................	1	8	8

B

	Article	Section	Clause
Bail. Excessive bail shall not be required, nor excessive fines nor cruel and unusual punishments imposed. [Amendments]	8	—	—
Ballot for President and Vice President. The electors shall vote by. [Amendments]	12	—	—
Ballot. If no person have a majority of the electoral votes for President and Vice President, the House of Representatives shall immediately choose the President by. [Amendments]..	12	—	—
Bankruptcies. Congress shall have power to pass uniform laws on the subject of........................	1	8	4
Basis of representation among the several States. Provisions relating to the. [Amendments]	14	2	—
Bear arms shall not be infringed. A well-regulated militia being necessary to the security of a free State, the right of the people to keep and. [Amendments]...	2	—	—
Behavior. The judges of the Supreme and inferior courts shall hold their offices during good	3	1	—
Bill of attainder or *ex post facto* law shall be passed. No	1	9	3
Bill of attainder, *ex post facto* law, or law impairing the obligation of contracts. No State shall pass any..	1	10	1
Bills of credit. No State shall emit......................	1	10	1

	Article	Section	Clause
Bills for raising revenue shall originate in the House of Representatives. All	1	7	1
Bills which shall have passed the Senate and House of Representatives shall, before they become laws, be presented to the President....	1	7	2
If he approve, he shall sign them: if he disapprove, he shall return them, with his objections, to that House in which they originated...	1	7	2
Upon the reconsideration of a bill returned by the President with his objections, if two-thirds of each House agree to pass the same, it shall become a law	1	7	2
Upon the reconsideration of a bill returned by the President, the question shall be taken by yeas and nays..	1	7	2
Not returned by the President within ten days (Sundays excepted) shall, unless Congress adjourn, become laws.......................	1	7	2
Borrow money on the credit of the United States. Congress shall have power to..........................	1	8	2
Bounties and pensions, shall not be questioned. The validity of the public debt incurred in suppressing insurrection and rebellion against the United States, including the debt for. [Amendments]	14	4	—
Breach of the peace, shall be privileged from arrest while attending the session, and in going to and returning from the same. Senators and Representatives, except for treason, felony, and	1	6	1
Bribery, or other high crimes and misdemeanors. The President, Vice President, and all civil officers shall be removed on impeachment for and conviction of treason	2	4	—

	Article	Section	Clause
Neither House, during the session of Congress, shall, without the consent of the other, adjourn for more than three days......	1	5	4
Senators and Representatives shall receive a compensation to be ascertained by law	1	6	1
They shall in all cases, except treason, felony, and breach of peace, be privileged from arrest during attendance at their respective Houses, and in going to and returning from the same	1	6	1
No Senator or Representative shall, during his term, be appointed to any civil office which shall have been created, or of which the emoluments shall have been increased, during such term..	1	6	2
No person holding any office under the United States, shall, while in office, be a member of either House of Congress..........	1	6	2
All bills for raising revenue shall originate in the House of Representatives....................	1	7	1
Proceedings in cases of bills returned by the President with his objections.....................	1	7	2
Shall have power to lay and collect duties, imposts, and excises, pay the debts, and provide for the common defense and general welfare...	1	8	1
Shall have power to borrow money on the credit of the United States	1	8	2
To regulate foreign and domestic commerce, and with the Indian tribes..........................	1	8	3
To establish uniform rule of naturalization and uniform laws on the subject of bankruptcies.....................................	1	8	4
To coin money, regulate its value and the value of foreign coin, and to fix the standard of weights and measures..........................	1	8	5
To punish counterfeiting of securities and current coin of the United States...............	1	8	6

	Article	Section	Clause
To establish post-offices and post-roads........	1	8	7
To promote the progress of science and the useful arts..	1	8	8
To constitute tribunals inferior to the Supreme Court	1	8	9
To define and punish piracies and felonies on the high seas and to punish offenses against the law of nations	1	8	10
To declare war, grant letters of marque and reprisal, and make rules concerning captures on land and water.............................	1	8	11
To raise and support armies, but no appropriation of money to that use shall be for a longer term than two years	1	8	12
To provide and maintain a Navy......................	1	8	13
To make rules for the government of the Army and Navy	1	8	14
To call out the militia to execute the laws, suppress insurrections, and repeal invasions	1	8	15
To provide for organizing, arming, and equipping the militia..	1	8	16
To exercise exclusive legislation over the District fixed for the seat of government, and over forts, magazines, arsenals, and dockyards...	1	8	17
To make all laws necessary and proper to carry into execution all powers vested by the Constitution in the Government of the United States	1	8	18
No person holding any office under the United States shall accept of any present, emolument, office, or title of any kind from any foreign state, without the consent of ...	1	9	8

	Article	Section	Clause
May determine the time of choosing the electors for President and Vice President and the day on which they shall give their votes..........	2	1	4
The President may, on extraordinary occasions, convene either House of	2	3	—
The manner in which the acts, records, and judicial proceedings of the States shall be prescribed by	4	1	—
New States may be admitted by Congress into this Union	4	3	1
Shall have power to make all needful rules and regulations respecting the territory or other property belonging to the United States	4	3	2
Amendments to the Constitution shall be proposed whenever it shall be deemed necessary by two-thirds of both Houses of.......	5	—	—
Shall have power to enforce, by appropriate legislation, the thirteenth amendment. [Amendments]	13	2	—
Persons engaged in insurrection or rebellion against the United States disqualified for Senators or Representatives in. [Amendments]	14	3	—
But such disqualification may be removed by a vote of two-thirds of both Houses of. [Amendments]	14	3	—
Shall have power to enforce, by appropriate legislation, the fourteenth amendment. [Amendments]	14	5	—
Shall have power to enforce, by appropriate legislation, the fifteenth amendment. [Amendments]	15	2	—
Shall have power to enforce, by appropriate legislation, the nineteenth amendment. [Amendments]	19	—	—
Sessions, time of assembling. [Amendments]	20	2	—

	Article	Section	Clause
No State shall enter into any agreement or compact with another State, or with a foreign power, without the	1	10	3
No State shall engage in war unless actually invaded, or in such imminent danger as will not admit of delay, without the	1	10	3
No new State shall be formed or erected within the jurisdiction of any other State, nor any State formed by the junction of two or more States, or parts of States, without the consent of the legislatures thereof, as well as the..............................	4	3	1
Consent of the legislature of the State in which the same may be. Congress shall exercise exclusive authority over all places purchased for the erection of forts, magazines, arsenals, dockyards, and other needful buildings by the ..	1	8	17
Consent of the legislatures of the States and of Congress. No States shall be formed by the junction of two or more States or parts of States without the...	4	3	1
Consent of the other. Neither House, during the session of Congress, shall adjourn for more than three days, nor to any other place than that in which they shall be sitting, without the	1	5	4
Consent of the owner. No soldier shall be quartered in time of peace in any house without the. [Amendments]...	3	—	—
Consent of the Senate. The President shall have power to make treaties, by and with the advice and	2	2	2
The President shall appoint ambassadors, other public ministers and consuls, judges of the Supreme Court, and all other officers created by law and not otherwise herein provided for, by and with the advice and.....	2	2	2

	Article	Section	Clause
Constitution, in the Government of the United States, or in any department or officer thereof. Congress shall have power to pass all laws necessary to the execution of the powers vested by the..	1	8	18
Constitution, shall be eligible to the office of President. No person except a natural-born citizen, or a citizen at the time of the adoption of the	2	1	5
Constitution. The President, before he enters upon the execution of his office, shall take an oath to preserve, protect, and defend the	2	1	8
Constitution, laws, and treaties of the United States. The judicial power shall extend to all cases arising under the....................................	3	2	1
Constitution shall be so construed as to prejudice any claims of the United States, or of any State (in respect to territory or other property of the United States). Nothing in the	4	3	2
Constitution. The manner in which amendments may be proposed and ratified...........................	5	—	—
Constitution as under the Confederation shall be valid. All debts and engagements contracted before the adoption of the..............................	6	—	1
Constitution and the laws made in pursuance thereof, and all treaties made, or which shall be made, by the United States, shall be the supreme law of the land. The...........................	6	—	2
The judges in every State, anything in the constitution or laws of a State to the contrary notwithstanding, shall be bound thereby	6	—	2
Constitution. All officers, legislative, executive, and judicial, of the United States, and of the several States, shall be bound by an oath to support the	6	—	3

	Article	Section	Clause
Debts and engagements contracted before the adoption of this Constitution shall be as valid against the United States, under it, as under the Confederation..	6	—	1
Debts or obligations incurred in aid of insurrection or rebellion against the United States, or claims for the loss or emancipation of any slave. Neither the United States nor any State shall assume or pay any. [Amendments]	14	4	—
Declare war, grant letters of marque and reprisal, and make rules concerning captures on land and water. Congress shall have power to	1	8	11
Defense, promote the general welfare, &c. To insure the common. [Preamble].......................	—	—	—
Defense and general welfare throughout the United States. Congress shall have power to pay the debts and provide for the common.......	1	8	1
Defense. In all criminal prosecutions the accused shall have the assistance of counsel for his. [Amendments]	6	—	—
Delaware entitled to one Representative in the first Congress..	1	2	3
Delay. No State shall, without the consent of Congress, engage in war unless actually invaded, or in such imminent danger as will not admit of	1	10	3
Delegated to the United States, nor prohibited to the States, are reserved to the States or to the people. The powers not. [Amendments]...........	10	—	—
Deny or disparage others retained by the people. The enumeration in the Constitution of certain rights shall not be construed to. [Amendments]	9	—	—
Departments upon any subject relating to their duties. The President may require the written opinion of the principal officers in each of the executive	2	2	1

	Article	Section	Clause
Departments. Congress may by law vest the appointment of inferior officers in the heads of....	2	2	2
Direct tax shall be laid unless in proportion to the census or enumeration. No capitation or other..	1	9	4
Direct taxes and Representatives, how apportioned among the several States......................	1	2	3
Disability of the President and Vice President. Provisions in case of the	2	1	6
[Amendments]...	25	—	—
Disability. No person shall be a Senator or Representative in Congress, or presidential elector, or hold any office, civil or military, under the United States, or any State, who having previously taken an oath as a legislative, executive, or judicial officer of the United States, or of any State, to support the Constitution, afterward engaged in insurrection or rebellion against the United States. [Amendments]	14	3	—
But Congress may, by a vote of two-thirds of each House, remove such. [Amendments]..	14	3	—
Disagreement between the two Houses as to the time of adjournment, the President may adjourn them to such time as he may think proper. In case of...	2	3	—
Disorderly behavior. Each House may punish its members for...	1	5	2
And with the concurrence of two-thirds expel a member	1	5	2
Disparage others retained by the people. The enumeration in the Constitution of certain rights shall not be construed to deny or. [Amendments]...	9	—	—
Disqualification. No Senator or Representative shall, during the time for which he was elected, be appointed to any office under the United States which shall have been created or its emoluments increased during such term..........	1	6	2

	Article	Section	Clause
No person holding any office under the United States shall be a member of either House during his continuance in office.......	1	6	2
No person shall be a member of either House, presidential elector, or hold any office under the United States, or any State, who, having previously sworn to support the Constitution, afterward engaged in insurrection or rebellion. [Amendments]	14	3	—
But Congress may, by a vote of two-thirds of each House, remove such disability. [Amendments]	14	3	—
District of Columbia. Congress shall exercise exclusive legislation in all cases over the	1	8	17
Electors for President and Vice President, appointment in such manner as the Congress may direct. [Amendments]	23	1	—
Dockyards. Congress shall have exclusive authority over all places purchased for the erection of	1	8	17
Domestic tranquility, provide for the common defense, &c. To insure. [Preamble]	—	—	—
Domestic violence. The United States shall protect each State against invasion and..............	4	4	—
Due process of law. No person shall be compelled, in any criminal case, to be a witness against himself, nor be deprived of life, liberty, or property without. [Amendments]	5	—	—
No State shall deprive any person of life, liberty, or property without. [Amendments]....	14	1	—
Duties, imposts, and excises. Congress shall have power to lay and collect taxes.................	1	8	1
Shall be uniform throughout the United States	1	8	1
Duties shall be laid on articles exported from any State. No tax or...	1	9	5

	Article	Section	Clause
But Congress may, at any time, alter such regulations, except as to the places of choosing Senators	1	4	1
Returns and qualifications of its own members. Each House shall be the judge of the.	1	5	1
Senators elected by the people. [Amendments]	17	1	—
Electors for members of the House of Representatives. Qualifications of	1	2	1
Electors for Senators. Qualifications of. [Amendments]	17	1	—
Electors for President and Vice President. Each State shall appoint, in such manner as the legislature thereof may direct, a number of electors equal to the whole number of Senators and Representatives to which the State may be entitled in the Congress	2	1	2
But no Senator or Representative, or person holding an office of trust or profit under the United States, shall be appointed an elector..	2	1	2
Congress may determine the time of choosing the electors and the day on which they shall give their votes.................................	2	1	4
Which day shall be the same throughout the United States	2	1	4
The electors shall meet in their respective States and vote by ballot for President and Vice President, one of whom, at least, shall not be an inhabitant of the same State with themselves. [Amendments]...............	12	—	—
The District of Columbia to appoint, in such manner as the Congress may direct, a number of electors equal to the whole number of Senators and Representatives to which the District would be entitled if a State. [Amendments]..	23	1	—

F

	Article	Section	Clause
Felonies committed on the high seas. Congress shall have power to define and punish piracies and	1	8	10
Felony, and breach of the peace. Members of Congress shall not be privileged from arrest for treason	1	6	1
Fines. Excessive fines shall not be imposed. [Amendments].....................................	8	—	—
Foreign coin. Congress shall have power to coin money, fix the standard of weights and measures, and to regulate the value of	1	8	5
Foreign nations, among the States, and with the Indian tribes. Congress shall have power to regulate commerce with	1	8	3
Foreign power. No State shall, without the consent of Congress, enter into any compact or agreement with any	1	10	3
Forfeiture, except during the life of the person attainted. Attainder of treason shall not work ..	3	3	2
Form of government. The United States shall guarantee to every State in this Union a republican..	4	4	—
And shall protect each of them against invasion; and on application of the legislature or of the executive (when the legislature cannot be convened), against domestic violence..	4	4	—
Formation of new States. Provisions relating to the...	4	3	1
Forts, magazines, arsenals, dock-yards, and other needful buildings. Congress shall exercise exclusive authority over all places purchased for the erection of..	1	8	17
Free State, the right of the people to keep and bear arms shall not be infringed. A well-regulated militia being necessary to the security of a. [Amendments]..	2	—	—

	Article	Section	Clause
Freedom of speech or the press. Congress shall make no law abridging the. [Amendments]	1	—	—
Fugitives from crime found in another State shall, on demand, be delivered up to the authorities of the State from which they may flee	4	2	2
Fugitives from service or labor in one State, escaping into another State, shall be delivered up to the party to whom such service or labor may be due..	4	2	3

G

	Article	Section	Clause
General welfare and secure the blessings of liberty, &c. To promote the. [Preamble.]..............	—	—	—
General welfare. Congress shall have power to provide for the common defense and	1	8	1
Georgia entitled to three Representatives in the first Congress....................................	1	2	3
Gold and silver coin a tender in payment of debts. No State shall make anything but..........	1	10	1
Good behavior. The judges of the Supreme and inferior courts shall hold their offices during	3	1	—
Government. The United States shall guarantee to every State in this Union a republican form of...	4	4	—
And shall protect each of them against invasion, and on application of the legislature or of the executive (when the legislature cannot be convened) against domestic violence...	4	4	—
Grand jury. No person shall be held to answer for a capital or otherwise infamous crime, unless on the presentment of a. [Amendments]..........	5	—	—
Except in cases arising in the land and naval forces, and in the militia when in actual service. [Amendments]	5	—	—
Guarantee to every State in this Union a republican form of government. The United States shall...	4	4	—

	Article	Section	Clause
And shall protect each of them against invasion; and on application of the legislature or of the executive (when the legislature cannot be convened), against domestic violence....................................	4	4	—

H

	Article	Section	Clause
Habeas corpus shall not be suspended unless in cases of rebellion or invasion. The writ of	1	9	2
Heads of departments. Congress may, by law, vest the appointment of inferior officers in the .	2	2	2
On any subject relating to their duties, the President may require the written opinion of the principal officers in each of the executive departments	2	2	1
High crimes and misdemeanors. The President, Vice President, and all civil officers shall be removed on impeachment for and conviction of treason, bribery, or other	2	4	—
House of Representatives. Congress shall consist of a Senate and..	1	1	—
Shall be composed of members chosen every second year...	1	2	1
Qualifications of electors for members of the	1	2	1
No person shall be a member who shall not have attained the age of twenty-five years, and been seven years a citizen of the United States	1	2	2
The executives of the several States shall issue writs of election to fill vacancies in the	1	2	4
Shall choose their Speaker and other officers	1	2	5
Shall have the sole power of impeachment....	1	2	5
Shall be the judge of the elections, returns, and qualifications of its own members	1	5	1
A majority shall constitute a quorum to do business..	1	5	1

	Article	Section	Clause
No person having as a legislative, executive, or judicial officer of the United States, or of any State, taken an oath to support the Constitution, and afterwards engaged in insurrection or rebellion against the United States, shall be a member of the. [Amendments]	14	3	—
But Congress may, by a vote of two-thirds of each house, remove such disability. [Amendments]	14	3	—

I

	Article	Section	Clause
Imminent danger as will not admit of delay. No State shall, without the consent of Congress, engage in war, unless actually invaded or in such..	1	10	3
Immunities. Members of Congress shall, in all cases except treason, felony, and breach of the peace, be privileged from arrest during their attendance at the session of their respective houses, and in going and returning from the same..	1	6	1
No soldier shall be quartered in any house without the consent of the owner in time of peace. [Amendments]	3	—	—
No person shall be twice put in jeopardy of life and limb for the same offense. [Amendments]	5	—	—
All persons born or naturalized in the United States, and subject to the jurisdiction thereof, are citizens of the United States and of the State in which they reside. [Amendments]	14	1	—
No State shall make or enforce any law which shall abridge the privileges or immunities of citizens of the United States. [Amendments]	14	1	—

	Article	Section	Clause
Nor shall any State deprive any person of life, liberty, or property without due process of law. [Amendments]	14	1	—
Nor deny to any person within its jurisdiction the equal protection of the law. [Amendments]	14	1	—
Impeachment. The President may grant reprieves and pardons except in cases of	2	2	1
The House of Representatives shall have the sole power of	1	2	5
Impeachment for and conviction of treason, bribery, and other high crimes and misdemeanors. The President, Vice President, and all civil officers shall be removed upon	2	4	—
Impeachments. The Senate shall have the sole power to try all	1	3	6
The Senate shall be on oath, or affirmation, when sitting for the trial of	1	3	6
When the President of the United States is tried the Chief Justice shall preside	1	3	6
No person shall be convicted without the concurrence of two-thirds of the members present	1	3	6
Judgment shall not extend beyond removal from office and disqualification to hold office	1	3	7
But the party convicted shall be liable to indictment and punishment according to law	1	3	7
Importation of slaves prior to 1808 shall not be prohibited by the Congress.............................	1	9	1
But a tax or duty of ten dollars for each person may be imposed on such	1	9	1
Imports or exports except what may be absolutely necessary for executing its inspection laws. No State shall, without the consent of Congress, lay any imposts or duties on	1	10	2

	Article	Section	Clause
Imports or exports laid by any State shall be for the use of the Treasury. The net produce of all duties on...	1	10	2
Imports or exports shall be subject to the revision and control of Congress. All laws of States laying duties on	1	10	2
Imposts and excises. Congress shall have power to lay and collect taxes, duties	1	8	1
Shall be uniform throughout the United States. All taxes, duties............................	1	8	1
Inability of the President. The powers and duties of his office shall devolve on the Vice President. In case of the death, resignation, or........	2	1	6
[Amendments]...	25	—	—
The Vice President shall succeed to the office of the President. In case of the death, resignation, or removal, or [Amendments] ..	25	—	—
Inability of the President or Vice President. Congress may provide by law for the case of the removal, death, resignation, or	2	1	6
[Amendments]...	25	—	—
Income taxes. Congress shall have power to lay and collect without apportionment among the several States, and without regard to any census or enumeration. [Amendments]	16	—	—
Indian tribes. Congress shall have power to regulate commerce with the	1	8	3
Indictment or presentment of a grand jury. No person shall be held to answer for a capital or infamous crime unless on [Amendments].........	5	—	—
Except in cases arising in the land and naval forces, and in the militia when in actual service. [Amendments]	5	—	—
Indictment, trial, judgment, and punishment, according to law. The party convicted in case of impeachment shall nevertheless be liable and subject to...	1	3	7

	Article	Section	Clause
Infamous crime unless on presentment or indictment of a grand jury. No person shall be held to answer for a capital or [Amendments]	5	—	—
Inferior courts. Congress shall have power to constitute tribunals inferior to the Supreme Court	1	8	9
Inferior courts as Congress may establish. The judicial power of the United States shall be vested in one Supreme Court and such............	3	1	—
The judges of both the Supreme and inferior courts shall hold their offices during good behavior	3	1	—
Their compensation shall not be diminished during their continuance in office..............	3	1	—
Inferior officers, Congress, if they think proper, may by law vest the appointment of in the President alone, in the courts of law, or in the heads of Departments......................................	2	2	2
Inhabitant of the State for which he shall be chosen. No person shall be a Senator who shall not have attained the age of thirty years, been nine years a citizen of the United States, and who shall not, when elected, be an..................	1	3	3
Insurrection or rebellion against the United States. No person shall be a Senator or Representative in Congress, or presidential elector, or hold any office, civil or military, under the United States, or any State, who, having taken an oath as a legislative, executive, or judicial officer of the United States, or of a State, afterwards engaged in. [Amendments]	14	3	—
But Congress may, by a vote of two-thirds of each House, remove such disabilities. [Amendments]	14	3	—
Debts declared illegal and void which were contracted in aid of. [Amendments]...........	14	4	—
Insurrections and repel invasions. Congress shall provide for calling forth the militia to suppress	1	8	15

	Article	Section	Clause
Legislation. Congress shall have power to make all laws necessary and proper for carrying into execution all the powers vested by the Constitution in the Government of the United States or in any department or officer thereof............	1	8	18
Congress shall have power to enforce the thirteenth amendment, prohibiting slavery, by appropriate. [Amendments]..................	13	2	—
Congress shall have power to enforce the fourteenth amendment by appropriate. [Amendments]..	14	5	—
Congress shall have power to enforce the fifteenth amendment by appropriate. [Amendments]	15	2	—
Congress and the several States shall have concurrent power to enforce the eighteenth amendment by appropriate. [Amendments]	18	2	—
Congress shall have power to enforce the nineteenth amendment by appropriate. [Amendments]..	19	—	—
Congress shall have power to enforce the twenty-third amendment by appropriate. [Amendments]..	23	2	—
Congress shall have power to enforce the twenty-fourth amendment by appropriate. [Amendments]..	24	2	—
Congress shall have power to enforce the twenty-sixth amendment by appropriate. [Amendments]..	26	2	—
Legislative powers herein granted shall be vested in Congress. All..	1	1	—
Legislature, or the Executive (when the legislature cannot be convened). The United States shall protect each State against invasion and domestic violence, on the application of the	4	4	—

	Article	Section	Clause
Legislatures of two-thirds of the States, Congress shall call a convention for proposing amendments to the Constitution. On the application of the....................................	5	—	—
Letters of marque and reprisal. Congress shall have power to grant	1	8	11
No State shall grant	1	10	1
Liberty to ourselves and our posterity, &c. To secure the blessings of. [Preamble]	—	—	—
Life or limb for the same offense. No person shall be twice put in jeopardy of. [Amendments]	5	—	—
Life, liberty, and property without due process of law. No person shall be compelled in any criminal case to be a witness against himself, nor be deprived of. [Amendments].........................	5	—	—
No State shall abridge the privileges or immunities of citizens of the United States, nor deprive any person of. [Amendments] ..	14	1	—
Loss or emancipation of any slave shall be held illegal and void. Claims for the. [Amendments]	14	4	—

M

	Article	Section	Clause
Magazines, arsenals, dock-yards, and other needful buildings. Congress shall have exclusive authority over all places purchased for the erection of..	1	8	17
Majority of each House shall constitute a quorum to do business. A	1	5	1
But a smaller number may adjourn from day to day and may be authorized to compel the attendance of absent members...........	1	5	1
Majority of all the States shall be necessary to a choice. When the choice of a President shall devolve on the House of Representatives, a quorum shall consist of a member or members from two-thirds of the States; but a [Amendments]	12	—	—

	Article	Section	Clause
Naturalization. Congress shall have power to establish a uniform rule of	1	8	4
Naturalized in the United States, and subject to their jurisdiction, shall be citizens of the United States and of the States in which they reside. All persons born, or. [Amendments]	14	1	—
Naval forces. Congress shall make rules and regulations for the government and regulation of the land and	1	8	14
Navy. Congress shall have power to provide and maintain a	1	8	13
New Hampshire entitled to three Representatives in the first Congress	1	2	3
New Jersey entitled to four Representatives in the first Congress	1	2	3
New States may be admitted by Congress into this Union	4	3	1
But no new State shall be formed within the jurisdiction of another State without the consent of Congress	4	3	1
Nor shall any State be formed by the junction of two or more States or parts of States, without the consent of the legislatures and of Congress	4	3	1
New York entitled to six Representatives in the first Congress	1	2	3
Nobility shall be granted by the United States. No title of	1	9	8
No State shall grant any title of	1	10	1
Nominations for office by the President. The President shall nominate, and, by and with the advice and consent of the Senate, shall appoint ambassadors and other public officers	2	2	2
He may grant commissions to fill vacancies that happen in the recess of the Senate, which shall expire at the end of their next session	2	2	3

	Article	Section	Clause
Persons, as any State may think proper to admit, shall not be prohibited prior to 1808. The migration or importation of such	1	9	1
But a tax or duty of ten dollars shall be imposed on the importation of each of such ..	1	9	1
Petition for the redress of grievances. Congress shall make no law abridging the right of the people peaceably to assemble and to. [Amendments]	1	—	—
Piracies and felonies committed on the high seas. Congress shall define and punish............	1	8	10
Place than that in which the two Houses shall be sitting. Neither House during the session shall, without the consent of the other, adjourn for more than three days, nor to any other	1	5	4
Places of choosing Senators. Congress may by law make or alter regulations for the election of Senators and Representatives, except as to the...	1	4	1
Poll tax. The right of citizens of the United States to vote shall not be denied or abridged by the United States or any State by reason of failure to pay. [Amendments]	24	1	—
Ports of one State over those of another. Preference shall not be given by any regulation of commerce or revenue to the...........................	1	9	6
Vessels clearing from the ports of one State shall not pay duties in another...................	1	9	6
Post offices and post roads. Congress shall establish...	1	8	7
Powers herein granted shall be vested in Congress. All legislative	1	1	—
Powers vested by the Constitution in the Government or in any Department or officer of the United States. Congress shall make all laws necessary to carry into execution the	1	8	18

	Article	Section	Clause
Before he enters upon the execution of his office he shall take an oath of office	2	1	8
Shall be Commander in Chief of the Army and Navy and of the militia of the States when called into actual service	2	2	1
He may require the opinion, in writing, of the principal officer in each of the Executive Departments..	2	2	1
He may grant reprieves or pardons for offenses, except in cases of impeachment....	2	2	1
He may make treaties by and with the advice and consent of the Senate, two-thirds of the Senators present concurring...............	2	2	2
He may appoint, by and with the advice and consent of the Senate, ambassadors, other public ministers and consuls, judges of the Supreme Court, and all other officers whose appointments may be authorized by law and not herein provided for..................	2	2	2
Congress may vest the appointment of inferior officers in the	2	2	2
He may fill up all vacancies that may happen in the recess of the Senate by commissions which shall expire at the end of their next session	2	2	3
He shall give information to Congress of the state of the Union, and recommend measures...	2	3	—
On extraordinary occasions he may convene both Houses or either.................................	2	3	—
In case of disagreement between the two Houses as to the time of adjournment, he may adjourn them to such time as he may think proper..	2	3	—
He shall receive ambassadors and other public ministers...	2	3	—

	Article	Section	Clause
No Senator or Representative or person holding an office of trust or profit under the United States shall be an elector..............	2	1	2
Congress may determine the time of choosing the electors and the day on which they shall give their votes, which day shall be the same throughout the United States	2	1	4
The electors shall meet in their respective States and vote by ballot for President and Vice President, one of whom, at least, shall not be an inhabitant of the same State with themselves. [Amendments]................	12	—	—
They shall name in distinct ballots the person voted for as President and the person voted for as Vice President. [Amendments]	12	—	—
They shall make distinct lists of the persons voted for as President and as Vice President, which they shall sign and certify and transmit sealed to the President of the Senate at the seat of government. [Amendments]	12	—	—
The President of the Senate shall, in the presence of the Senate and House of Representatives, open all the certificates, and the votes shall then be counted. [Amendments]	12	—	—
The person having the greatest number of votes shall be the President, if such number be a majority of the whole number of electors appointed. [Amendments]	12	—	—
If no person have such majority, then from the persons having the highest numbers, not exceeding three, on the list of those voted for as President, the House of Representatives shall choose immediately, by ballot, the President. [Amendments]..........	12	—	—
In choosing the President, the votes shall be taken by States, the representation from each State having one vote. [Amendments]	12	—	—

	Article	Section	Clause
No State shall make or enforce any law which shall abridge the privileges or immunities of citizens of the United States. [Amendments]	14	1	—
No State shall deprive any person of life, liberty, or property without due process of law. [Amendments]	14	1	—
Nor deny to any person within its jurisdiction the equal protection of its laws. [Amendments]	14	1	—
Prizes captured on land or water. Congress shall make rules concerning	1	8	11
Probable cause. The right of the people to be secure in their persons, houses, papers, and effects, against unreasonable searches and seizures, shall not be violated. And no warrant shall issue for such but upon. [Amendments]	4	—	—
Process for obtaining witnesses in his favor. In all criminal prosecutions the accused shall have. [Amendments]	6	—	—
Process of law. No person shall be compelled in any criminal case to be a witness against himself, nor be deprived of life, liberty, or property, without due. [Amendments]	5	—	—
No State shall deprive any person of life, liberty, or property, without due. [Amendments]	14	1	—
Progress of science and useful arts. Congress shall have power to promote the	1	8	8
Property of the United States. Congress may dispose of and make all needful rules and regulations respecting the territory or	4	3	3
Property, without due process of law. No person shall be compelled in any criminal case to be a witness against himself; nor shall he be deprived of his life, liberty, or. [Amendments]	5	—	—

	Article	Section	Clause
No State shall abridge the privileges or immunities of citizens of the United States; nor deprive any person of his life, liberty, or. [Amendments]	14	1	—
Prosecutions. The accused shall have a speedy and public trial in all criminal. [Amendments] ..	6	—	—
He shall be tried by a jury in the State or district where the crime was committed. [Amendments]	6	—	—
He shall be informed of the nature and cause of the accusation. [Amendments]	6	—	—
He shall be confronted with the witnesses against him. [Amendments]	6	—	—
He shall have compulsory process for obtaining witnesses. [Amendments]	6	—	—
He shall have counsel for his defense. [Amendments]	6	—	—
Protection of the laws. No State shall deny to any person within its jurisdiction the equal. [Amendments]	14	1	—
Public debt of the United States incurred in suppressing insurrection or rebellion shall not be questioned. The validity of the. [Amendments]	14	4	—
Public safety must require it. The writ of **habeas corpus** shall not be suspended, unless when in cases of rebellion or invasion the	1	9	2
Public trial by jury. In all criminal prosecutions the accused shall have a speedy and. [Amendments]	6	—	—
Public use. Private property shall not be taken for, without just compensation. [Amendments]	5	—	—
Punishment according to law. Judgment in cases of impeachment shall not extend further than to removal from, and disqualification for, office; but the party convicted shall nevertheless be liable and subject to indictment, trial, judgment, and	1	3	7

	Article	Section	Clause
Ratio of representation shall be apportioned among the several States according to their respective numbers, counting the whole number of persons in each State, excluding Indians not taxed. [Amendments]	14	2	—
But when the right to vote for Presidential electors or members of Congress, or the legislative, executive, and judicial officers of the State, except for engaging in rebellion or other crime, shall be denied or abridged by a State, the basis of representation shall be reduced therein in the proportion of such denial or abridgment of the right to vote. [Amendments]................	14	2	—
Rebellion against the United States. Persons who, while holding certain Federal and State offices, took an oath to support the Constitution, afterward engaged in insurrection or rebellion, disabled from holding office under the United States. [Amendments]	14	3	—
But Congress may by a vote of two-thirds of each House remove such disability. [Amendments]	14	3	—
Debts incurred for pensions and bounties for services in suppressing the rebellion shall not be questioned. [Amendments]	14	4	—
All debts and obligations incurred in aid of the rebellion, and all claims for the loss or emancipation of slaves, declared and held to be illegal and void. [Amendments].........	14	4	—
Rebellion or invasion. The writ of habeas corpus shall not be suspended except when the public safety may require it in cases of......................	1	9	2
Receipts and expenditures of all public money shall be published from time to time. A regular statement of	1	9	7

	Article	Section	Clause
Representation. No State, without its consent, shall be deprived of its equal suffrage in the Senate	5	—	—
Representation and direct taxation, how apportioned among the several States	1	2	3
Representation until the first enumeration under the Constitution not to exceed one for every thirty thousand. The ratio of	1	2	3
Representation in any State. The executive thereof shall issue writs of election to fill vacancies in the	1	2	4
Representation among the several States shall be according to their respective numbers, counting the whole number of persons in each State, excluding Indians not taxed. The ratio of. [Amendments]	14	2	—
But where the right to vote in certain Federal and State elections is abridged for any cause other than rebellion or other crime, the basis of representation shall be reduced. [Amendments]	14	2	—
Representatives. Congress shall consist of a Senate and House of	1	1	—
Qualifications of electors of members of the House of	1	2	1
No person shall be a Representative who shall not have attained the age of twenty-five years, been seven years a citizen of the United States, and an inhabitant of the State in which he shall be chosen	1	2	2
And direct taxes, how apportioned among the several States	1	2	3
Executives of the State shall issue writs of election to fill vacancies in the House of	1	2	4
Shall choose their Speaker and other officers. The House of	1	2	5
Shall have the sole power of impeachment. The House of	1	2	5

	Article	Section	Clause
The times, places, and manner of choosing Representatives shall be prescribed by the legislatures of the States	1	4	1
But Congress may make by law at any time or alter such regulations except as to the places of choosing Senators......................	1	4	1
And Senators shall receive a compensation, to be ascertained by law	1	6	1
Shall in all cases, except treason, felony, and breach of the peace, be privileged from arrest during attendance at the session of the House, and in going to and returning from the same	1	6	1
Shall not be questioned in any other place for any speech or debate. Members of the House of..	1	6	1
No member shall be appointed during his term to any civil office which shall have been created, or the emoluments of which shall have been increased, during such term..	1	6	2
No person holding any office under the United States shall, while holding such office, be a member of the House of.....................	1	6	2
All bills for raising revenue shall originate in the House of..	1	7	1
No Senator or Representative shall be an elector for President or Vice President.......	2	1	2
No law, varying the compensation for the services of the Senators and Representatives, shall take effect, until an election of Representatives shall have intervened. [Amendments]	27	—	—
Representatives shall be bound by an oath or affirmation to support the Constitution of the United States. The Senators and.....................	6	—	3

	Article	Section	Clause
Representatives among the several States. Provisions relative to the apportionment of. [Amendments]..................	14	2	—
Representatives and Senators. Prescribing certain disqualifications for office as. [Amendments]..........................	14	3	—
But Congress may, by a vote of two-thirds of each House, remove such disqualification. [Amendments]..........................	14	3	—
Reprieves and pardons except in cases of impeachment. The President may grant..............	2	2	1
Reprisal. Congress shall have power to grant letters of marque and..........................	1	8	11
No State shall grant any letters of marque and..........................	1	10	1
Republican form of government. The United States shall guarantee to every State in this Union a	4	4	—
And shall protect each of them against invasion; and on the application of the legislature, or of the executive (when the legislature cannot be convened), against domestic violence......................	4	4	—
Reserved rights of the States and the people. The enumeration in the Constitution of certain rights shall not be construed to deny or disparage others retained by the people. [Amendments]..........................	9	—	—
The powers not delegated to the United States by the Constitution, nor prohibited by it to the States, are reserved to the States respectively, or to the people. [Amendments]..........................	10	—	—
Resignation of the President. The duties and powers of his office shall devolve on the Vice President. In case of the death	2	1	6
Congress may by law provide for the case of the removal, death	2	1	6

	Article	Section	Clause
The Vice President shall succeed to the office of the President. In case of the death, removal, inability, or [Amendments]	25	—	—
Resolution, or vote (except on a question of adjournment) requiring the concurrence of the two Houses shall, before it becomes a law, be presented to the President. Every order...........	1	7	3
Revenue shall originate in the House of Representatives. All bills for raising	1	7	1
Revenue. Preference shall not be given to the ports of one State over those of another by any regulations of commerce or.............................	1	9	6
Rhode Island entitled to one Representative in the first Congress...	1	2	3
Right of petition. Congress shall make no law abridging the right of the people peaceably to assemble and to petition for the redress of grievances. [Amendments].............................	1	—	—
Right to keep and bear arms. A well-regulated militia being necessary to the security of a free State, the right of the people to keep and bear arms shall not be infringed. [Amendments]......	2	—	—
Rights in the Constitution shall not be construed to deny or disparage others retained by the people. The enumeration of certain. [Amendments]	9	—	—
Rights not delegated to the United States nor prohibited to the States are reserved to the States or to the people. [Amendments]	10	—	—
Rules of its proceedings. Each House may determine the..	1	5	2
Rules and regulations respecting the territory or other property of the United States. Congress shall dispose of and make all needful...............	4	3	2
Rules of the common law. All suits involving over twenty dollars shall be tried by jury according to the. [Amendments].......................................	7	—	—

	Article	Section	Clause
No fact tried by a jury shall be re-examined except according to the. [Amendments]	7	—	—

S

	Article	Section	Clause
Science and the useful arts by securing to authors and inventors the exclusive right to their writings and discoveries. Congress shall have power to promote the progress of..................	1	8	8
Searches and seizures shall not be violated. The right of the people to be secure against unreasonable. [Amendments]	4	—	—
And no warrants shall be issued but upon probable cause, on oath or affirmation, describing the place to be searched and the persons or things to be seized. [Amendments]	4	—	—
Seat of Government. Congress shall exercise exclusive legislation in all cases over such district as may become the	1	8	17
Securities and current coin of the United States. Congress shall provide for punishing the counterfeiting of the	1	8	6
Security of a free State, the right of the people to keep and bear arms shall not be infringed. A well-regulated militia being necessary to the. [Amendments]..	2	—	—
Senate and House of Representatives. The Congress of the United States shall consist of a....	1	1	—
Senate of the United States. The Senate shall be composed of two Senators from each State, chosen by the legislature for six years.............	1	3	1
The Senate shall be composed of two Senators from each State, elected by the people thereof, for six years. [Amendments]	17	1	—
Qualifications of electors of Senators. [Amendments]...	17	1	—

	Article	Section	Clause
If vacancies happen during the recess of the legislature of a State, the executive thereof may make temporary appointments until the next meeting of the legislature	1	3	2
When vacancies happen the executive authority of the State shall issue writs of election to fill such vacancies; provided, that the legislature of any State may empower the executive thereof to make temporary appointment until the people fill the vacancies by election as the legislature may direct. [Amendments]	17	2	—
The Vice President shall be President of the Senate, but shall have no vote unless the Senate be equally divided...........................	1	3	4
The Senate shall choose their other officers, and also a President **pro tempore** in the absence of the Vice President or when he shall exercise the office of President	1	3	5
The Senate shall have the sole power to try all impeachments. When sitting for that purpose they shall be on oath or affirmation	1	3	6
When the President of the United States is tried the Chief Justice shall preside; and no person shall be convicted without the concurrence of two-thirds of the members present..	1	3	6
It shall be the judge of the elections, returns, and qualifications of its own members	1	5	1
A majority shall constitute a quorum to do business, but a smaller number may adjourn from day to day, and may be authorized to compel the attendance of absent members	1	5	1
It may determine the rules of its proceedings, punish a member for disorderly behavior, and with the concurrence of two-thirds expel a member	1	5	2

	Article	Section	Clause
It shall keep a journal of its proceedings and from time to time publish the same, except such parts as may in their judgment require secrecy	1	5	3
It shall not adjourn for more than three days during a session without the consent of the other House	1	5	4
It may propose amendments to bills for raising revenue, but such bills shall originate in the House of Representatives....................	1	7	1
The Senate shall advise and consent to the ratification of all treaties, provided two-thirds of the members present concur........	2	2	2
It shall advise and consent to the appointment of ambassadors, other public ministers and consuls, judges of the Supreme Court, and all other officers not herein otherwise provided for..............................	2	2	2
It may be convened by the President on extraordinary occasions...............................	2	3	1
No State, without its consent, shall be deprived of its equal suffrage in the Senate ...	5	—	—
Senators. They shall, immediately after assembling, under their first election, be divided into three classes, so that the seats of one-third shall become vacant at the expiration of every second year..	1	3	2
No person shall be a Senator who shall not be thirty years of age, nine years a citizen of the United States, and an inhabitant when elected of the State for which he shall be chosen...	1	3	3
The times, places, and manner of choosing Senators may be fixed by the legislature of a State, but Congress may by law make or alter such regulations, except as the places of choosing	1	4	1

	Article	Section	Clause
No person shall be a Senator or Representative who, having, as a Federal or State officer, taken an oath to support the Constitution, afterward engaged in rebellion against the United States. [Amendments]	14	3	—
But Congress may, by a vote of two-thirds of each House, remove such disability. [Amendments]	14	3	—
No law, varying the compensation for the services of the Senators and Representatives, shall take effect, until an election of Representatives shall have intervened. [Amendments]	27	—	—
Service or labor in one State, escaping into another State, shall be delivered up to the party to whom such service or labor may be due. Fugitives from	4	2	3
Servitude, except as a punishment for crime, whereof the party shall have been duly convicted, shall exist in the United States or any place subject to their jurisdiction. Neither slavery nor involuntary. [Amendments]	13	1	—
Servitude. The right of citizens of the United States to vote shall not be denied or abridged by the United States or by any State, on account of race, color, or previous condition of. [Amendments]	15	1	—
Sex. Right of citizens to vote shall not be denied or abridged by the United States or any State on account of. [Amendments]	19	—	—
Ships of war in time of peace, without the consent of Congress. No State shall keep troops or	1	10	3
Silver coin a tender in payment of debts. No State shall make anything but gold and	1	10	1

	Article	Section	Clause
State of the Union. The President shall, from time to time, give Congress information of the.	2	3	—
States. When vacancies happen in the representation from any State, the executive authority shall issue writs of election to fill such vacancies...	1	2	4
When vacancies happen in the representation of any State in the Senate, the executive authority shall issue writs of election to fill such vacancies. [Amendments]	17	2	—
Congress shall have power to regulate commerce among the several	1	8	3
No State shall enter into any treaty, alliance, or confederation...	1	10	1
Shall not grant letters of marque and reprisal	1	10	1
Shall not coin money....................................	1	10	1
Shall not emit bills of credit	1	10	1
Shall not make anything but gold and silver coin a tender in payment of debts..............	1	10	1
Shall not pass any bill of attainder, **ex post facto** law, or law impairing the obligation of contracts..	1	10	1
Shall not grant any title of nobility	1	10	1
Shall not, without the consent of Congress, lay any duties on imports or exports, except what may be absolutely necessary for executing its inspection laws	1	10	2
Shall not, without the consent of Congress, lay any duty of tonnage, keep troops or ships of war in time of peace, enter into any agreement or compact with another State or with a foreign power, or engage in war unless actually invaded or in such imminent danger as will not admit of delay	1	10	3
Full faith and credit in every other State shall be given to the public acts, records, and judicial proceedings of each State	4	1	—

	Article	Section	Clause
The compensation of the judges shall not be diminished during their continuance in office..	3	1	—
Shall have original jurisdiction. In all cases affecting ambassadors, other public ministers and consuls, and in which a State may be a party, the	3	2	2
Shall have appellate jurisdiction, both as to law and the fact, with such exceptions and regulations as Congress may make. The	3	2	2
Supreme law of the land. This Constitution, the laws made in pursuance thereof, and the treaties of the United States, shall be the..............	6	—	2
The judges in every State shall be bound thereby	6	—	2

T

	Article	Section	Clause
Tax shall be laid unless in proportion to the census or enumeration. No capitation or other direct	1	9	4
Tax on incomes authorized without apportionment among the several States, and without regard to any census or enumeration. [Amendments]	16	—	—
Tax or duty shall be laid on articles exported from any State. No...	1	9	5
Tax. The right of citizens of the United States to vote shall not be denied or abridged by the United States or any State by reason of failure to pay. [Amendments]......................................	24	1	—
Taxes (direct) and Representatives, how apportioned among the several States	1	2	3
Taxes, duties, imposts, and excises. Congress shall have power to lay......................................	1	8	1
They shall be uniform throughout the United States	1	8	1

	Article	Section	Clause
Temporary appointments until the next meeting of the legislature. If vacancies happen in the Senate in the recess of the legislature of a State, the executive of the State shall make ...	1	3	2
Tender in payment of debts. No State shall make anything but gold and silver coin a	1	10	1
Term for which he is elected. No Senator or Representative shall be appointed to any office under the United States which shall have been created or its emoluments increased during the..................	1	6	2
Term of office. President, not more than twice. [Amendments]................	22	—	—
Terms of four years. The President and Vice President shall hold their offices for the...........	2	1	1
Territory or other property of the United States. Congress shall dispose of and make all needful rules and regulations respecting the................	4	3	2
Test as a qualification for any office or public trust shall ever be required. No religious..........	6	—	3
Testimony of two witnesses to the same overt act, or on confession in open court. No person shall be convicted of treason except on the.....	3	3	1
Three-fourths of the legislatures of the States, or conventions in three-fourths of the States, as Congress shall prescribe, may ratify amendments to the Constitution	5	—	—
Tie. The Vice President shall have no vote unless the Senate be equally divided..........................	1	3	4
Times, places, and manner of holding elections for Senators and Representatives shall be prescribed in each State by the legislature thereof	1	4	1
But Congress may at any time by law make or alter such regulations, except as to the places of choosing Senators......................	1	4	1

	Article	Section	Clause
Treaties. The President shall have power, with the advice and consent of the Senate, provided two-thirds of the Senators present concur, to make..........	2	2	2
The judicial power shall extend to all cases arising under the Constitution, laws, and....	3	2	1
They shall be the supreme law of the land, and the judges in every State shall be bound thereby...........................	6	—	2
Treaty, alliance, or confederation. No State shall enter into any................................	1	10	1
Trial, judgment, and punishment according to law. Judgment in cases of impeachment shall not extend further than to removal from, and disqualification for, office; but the party convicted shall nevertheless be liable and subject to indictment................................	1	3	7
Trial by jury. All crimes, except in cases of impeachment, shall be tried by jury.....................	3	2	3
Such trial shall be held in the State within which the crime shall have been committed...........................	3	2	3
But when not committed within a State, the trial shall be at such a place as Congress may by law have directed	3	2	3
In all criminal prosecutions the accused shall have a speedy and public. [Amendments] ..	6	—	—
Suits at common law, when the amount exceeds $20, shall be by. [Amendments].......	7	—	—
Tribunals, inferior to the Supreme Court. Congress shall have power to constitute	1	8	9
Troops or ships of war in time of peace without the consent of Congress. No State shall keep..	1	10	3
Trust or profit under the United States, shall be an elector for President and Vice President. No Senator, Representative, or person holding any office of...	2	1	2

	Article	Section	Clause
Validity of the public debt incurred in suppressing insurrection against the United States, including debt for pensions and bounties, shall not be questioned. [Amendments]..................	14	4	—
Vessels bound to or from the ports of one State, shall not be obliged to enter, clear, or pay duties in another State......................................	1	9	6
Veto of a bill by the President. Proceedings of the two Houses upon the	1	7	2
Vice President of the United States shall be President of the Senate	1	3	4
He shall have no vote unless the Senate be equally divided......................................	1	3	4
The Senate shall choose a President *pro tempore* in the absence of the........................	1	3	5
He shall be chosen for the term of four years	2	1	1
The number and the manner of appointing electors for President and	2	1	2
In case of the removal, death, resignation, or inability of the President, the powers and duties of his office shall devolve on the......	2	1	6
[Amendments]...	25	—	—
Congress may provide by law for the case of the removal, death, resignation, or inability both of the President and	2	1	6
[Amendments]...	25	—	—
On impeachment for and conviction of treason, bribery, and other high crimes and misdemeanors, shall be removed from office. The...	2	4	—
Vice President. The manner of choosing the. The electors shall meet in their respective States and vote by ballot for President and Vice President, one of whom, at least, shall not be an inhabitant of the same State with themselves. [Amendments]...	12	—	—

	Article	Section	Clause
Right of citizens who are eighteen years of age or older to vote shall not be denied or abridged by the United States or any State, on account of age. [Amendments]	26	1	—
Vote of two-thirds. Each House may expel a member by a	1	5	2
A bill vetoed by the President may be re-passed in each House by a	1	7	2
No person shall be convicted on an impeachment except by a	1	3	6
Whenever both Houses shall deem it necessary, Congress may propose amendments to the Constitution by a	5	—	—
The President may make treaties with the advice and consent of the Senate, by a	2	2	2
Disabilities incurred by participation in insurrection or rebellion, may be relieved by Congress by a. [Amendments]	14	3	—

W

	Article	Section	Clause
War, grant letters of marque and reprisal, and make rules concerning captures on land and water. Congress shall have power to declare	1	8	11
For governing the land and naval forces. Congress shall have power to make rules and articles of	1	8	14
No State shall, without the consent of Congress, unless actually invaded, or in such imminent danger as will not admit of delay, engage in	1	10	3
War against the United States, adhering to their enemies, and giving them aid and comfort. Treason shall consist only in levying	3	3	1
Warrants shall issue but upon probable cause, on oath or affirmation, describing the place to be searched, and the person or things to be seized. No. [Amendments]	4	—	—

	Article	Section	Clause
Weights and measures. Congress shall fix the standard of..	1	8	5
Welfare and to secure the blessings of liberty, &c. To promote the general. [Preamble]	—	—	—
Welfare. Congress shall have power to provide for the common defense and general	1	8	1
Witness against himself. No person shall, in a criminal case, be compelled to be a. [Amendments]	5	—	—
Witnesses against him. In all criminal prosecutions the accused shall be confronted with the. [Amendments]..	6	—	—
Witnesses in his favor. In all criminal prosecutions the accused shall have compulsory process for obtaining. [Amendments]..................	6	—	—
Witnesses to the same overt act, or on confession in open court. No person shall be convicted of treason unless on the testimony of two...	3	3	1
Writ of habeas corpus shall not be suspended unless in case of rebellion or invasion the public safety may require it	1	9	2
Writs of election to fill vacancies in the representation of any State. The executives of the State shall issue..	1	2	4
Written opinion of the principal officer in each of the Executive Departments on any subject relating to the duties of his office. The President may require the	2	2	1

Y

	Article	Section	Clause
Yeas and nays of the members of either House shall, at the desire of one-fifth of those present, be entered on the journals........................	1	5	3
The votes of both Houses upon the reconsideration of a bill returned by the President with his objections shall be determined by .	1	7	2